The awakening of
spiritual awareness

Keith Loy

authorHOUSE®

AuthorHouse™ UK Ltd.
500 Avebury Boulevard
Central Milton Keynes, MK9 2BE
www.authorhouse.co.uk
Phone: 08001974150

First published by AuthorHouse 9/4/2009

ISBN: 978-1-4490-1455-1 (sc)

This book is printed on acid-free paper.

Contents

Introduction

Whenever I wrote my first book *'Finding Reality'*, I tried to give the reader a sense of how certain philosophies, teachings and personally held belief systems, can stand as impediments before the sheer simplicity of spiritual awakening. I have found that some of these tend to complicate it all, and make awakening appear like the crock of gold at the end of the rainbow, which as we all know, is forever out of reach. In that first book, I used the story of my own search to illustrate this. I tried to persuade the reader to move beyond these thought made pictures of 'reality', in order to discover the truth of *actual* Reality for themselves, which is devoid of all thought and its projections of belief and philosophy.

My intention was to simplify spiritual awakening, by trying to liberate the reader from the need for a teacher, philosophy or a set of beliefs, so that they could finally awaken to the truth of their own Reality with ease. I wanted the reader to know that spiritual Reality with absolute certainty, in their own experience. I quite literally desired to lead my readers _beyond belief_ in all respects!

1

However, after the publication of that first book, I received some feedback which only further confirmed for me, how a lot of spiritual seekers were content to read spiritual books indefinitely, and never *really* find that Reality which the books spoke of. I realized that spiritual seeking had become a hobby for these people; they were quite content to live with the entertainment gained through the thought content of their mind. I fully understood that these types would never *really* desire true spiritual awakening to occur - until of course, there came a point when they had grown weary of the thought world, which they dreamed within their mind. I found that there was no way either 'I' or any other, would ever persuade these people to pull back the veil of thought, to even dare to consider, that the awakening of spiritual awareness is so simple, whenever we are *truly* ready to move beyond thought, and its projected systems of philosophy and belief.

On the other hand, I also received some feedback which gave me much hope, as I eventually discovered that many other readers, were indeed, honestly *willing* to look beyond their thought made pictures of 'reality', in order to awaken with ease, to live in the present moment, where our Reality is to be truly found. So, I have written this book for those in this camp. It's for those who finally feel ready to awaken, here and now. It's for those who want the truth, and have grown weary of seeking and not finding. I have written this book in an attempt to dissolve the need for mere belief and philosophy, and to untangle the complicated and often heady philosophies many spiritual seekers become so addicted to. We need awakening to be kept simple and uncluttered, for it to ever have any lasting effect upon our awareness. I have tried my best herein, to demystify and simplify spiritual awakening, so it can finally be accessible to all.

So, if you now feel ready to let go of what you *think* you know, in order to arrive at a point where you will *really know*, then maybe what I have written herein can be of some assistance to you. However, I do not see myself as being a spiritual teacher per se. I merely wish to convey to you (the reader) the realization which I have hit upon, in the hope that it can be of some help with regards to your awakening.

Included within this book are two chapters I have called 'Dialogues', where I have included and addressed some of the many questions, correspondence and discussions I was hit with, after the publication of *'Finding Reality'*. I have included these dialogues because I feel that they will add a lot of extra clarity for the reader, and hopefully give a more comprehensive slant to the book, to undo any lingering confusion there may be surrounding spiritual awakening.

Now, before you begin, you might want to familiarize yourself, with some of the common and not so common terms I will be using within this book. These are as follows.

The Ego:

The ego as I refer to it is a collection of thoughts and beliefs, which one might hold about themselves. It is what we think and believe that we are, as opposed to realizing what we truly are. It is a spell of hypnotic thought, a false identity, a mask we wear to parade in front of the world. We have come to be hypnotized by this mask, as being what we are. It is this mask of ego, which we mistakenly refer to as '*me*'.

La La Land:

This is the state of mind of one who remains partially asleep and in a trance all day long - lost in daydreams and thought dramas. It is the thought world, rather than the Real world. Most people might recognize it better as cloud cuckoo land. It is an opaque screen of hypnotic thought and belief, which obscures, distorts and darkens ones perception of true Reality.

Sleepwalkers:

This is a term I use to describe those who are completely lost in La La Land. They are so lost within a spell of thought, they are unable to see what is, they usually only see what they *think* is. They live in a thought world, and not the Real world.

The Spirit:

This is what we really are. It is this which we awaken to, when we shake off La La Land and its false ego. This Spirit is thee Reality, and it holds the perception of the *Real* world. It is this Spirit which becomes free through Spiritual awakening.

Reality:

Whenever you see this word beginning with a capital 'R', then I am referring to the non-dual nature of our true Reality. It is the ultimate Reality which lye's beyond thought, belief and philosophy, and it is where our absolute Oneness and true holistic spiritual nature is to be found. This Reality has gone by many names, some of which include - The Tao, Nirvana, The Kingdom of Heaven or 'God'. This Reality is the ultimate truth of every living thing, and from this source we derive our being, our world and our entire universe.

1
A New Dawn

The caricature of awakening:

Whenever I first heard about spiritual awakening or enlightenment (whatever term you prefer), I was a young man in my very early twenties. I had heard many strange stories about awakening back then, and in my innocent mind these stories would always bedazzle me. They were so powerfully charged with magical and mystical overtones, that I kind of got swept away by the captivating mystery of it all. Upon hearing the stories (which usually sprang from the east), I was somewhat enticed by all of the promises which were made of eternal ecstatic bliss, intense peace and union with God. Naturally upon hearing these promises, I then desired very much to become spiritually awakened. To think that I could achieve this state of being, led me to devote myself exclusively to finding it.

But the western Christian world considered the likes of 'me' to be a miserable sinner with stains upon my soul. So I wondered; how could an ordinary kind of guy like 'me' ever be good enough for this realization, which I believed to be the highest of all 'achievements' in life? With every spiritual teaching I bombarded my mind with, it felt less and less likely that I would ever be ready, or indeed *worthy* enough for spiritual awakening. In fact, with every spiritual teacher I listened to, and with every spiritual book I read, it only really served to make me feel smaller (inferior) by the day, like I wasn't good enough, like I was sure to be a major disappointment in the eyes of God. All of the worlds' awakened guys <u>*appeared*</u> to be immensely wise, virtuous, unstained and to be living 'good', chaste and unsullied lives. This only made me feel like I was sitting upon the lowest step of humanity's stairway to Heaven, since I was certainly not 'great', unlike the awakened guys I had heard about.

Perhaps this is the same for you reading this book? Perhaps you too feel less than adequate for spiritual awakening, huh?

Nevertheless, I still dreamed of the day that I could 'become' enlightened or awakened. I fantasized about what it would be like, and what it *really* meant to be awakened. Now, admittedly, I was a very naive young chap back then. I figured that awakening would feel much like some sort of endless high, similar to a drug induced ecstatic state. I presumed that I could get my fix of spiritual awakening from a reliable spiritual guru, in the same manner as a junkie could get their fix of drugs from a reliable drug dealer. All I would have to do, would be to find a good reliable dealer (guru) who could provide me with 100% of pure quality 'wisdom'. I would then cross his palm with gold or silver, and the dealer (guru) would then dispense his wisdom. When I ingested the wisdom, I guessed that I would be readily able to shift into this trance like altered state of consciousness, and reside there buzzing in uninterrupted ecstatic spiritual bliss forever.

I had heard that apparently life from that moment forth would contain no more problems, as I would be permanently reeling in a spiritual stupor. As a result, I would be unable to live a normal life within a politically correct society due to my being permanently high (spiritually that is). Yes, my extreme intoxication with the Spirit of God would render me useless in the modern world, and I would then have no choice but to give up the material world and all its trappings.

Therefore, I held a picture in my mind that this would mean that, once awakened, I would have no choice but to move out of town and flit up into the mountains, to live a life similar to that of a hermits. I would have to live in a shack or a cave for the rest of my days, and rumour had it that it was required of awakened folk to also take a vow of poverty. If you were rich and you wanted to awaken spiritually, well then you would have to give away all of your money to the poor, so that you too could become poor. When you became poor 'they' supposed that God would love you a little more, and so you would then be graced with better 'luck' in your endeavour to 'become' awakened. Indeed 'they' say that God doesn't like any of us having any cash at all, especially the awakened amongst us.

Later in life, I realized that '*they*' appeared to say an awful lot of stuff which made no sense. At one time, I merely believed that it was my spiritual ignorance which made their words seem confusing, but no, as I turned out '*they*' were just talking a whole lot of old nonsense after all. Indeed 'they' (whoever 'they' were) always had their noses stuck into the affairs of others. 'They' always knew best, 'they' wrote the rules concerning everything in life and 'they' were always right and you were always wrong. If one found oneself interested in anything at all in life (including awakening), one would have to endure a whole lot of folk telling one what 'they' had to say about it.

When it came to awakening, 'they' had a list of rules and regulations, do's and don'ts, lines to toe and traditions to upkeep. 'They' didn't approve of anyone paddling their own canoe, or breaking out of the accepted norms surrounding awakening either. If you found yourself questioning the validity of the teachings or methods 'they' laid down, well then you were either frowned upon, tabooed or called 'negative'. But nobody ever seemed to ask where 'they' got their information from, or just how credible it was. But as it happened, way back then, I, like the rest of humanity, unquestioningly accepted what 'they' had to say anyway – *Oh poor fool me!*

Now one of the *many* falsities which 'they' laid down concerning awakening, was the premise that awakened guys had to renounce worldly life. If you desired to live an ordinary life within society, then you would be called a 'worldly' person. Now, there was no way an ardent spiritual seeker like myself wanted to be labelled as being a 'worldly' person, so I, for a long time, bought into this renunciate mindset. Like I said, I was very naive. I was rather confident back then that I could certainly renounce the worldly lifestyle if it came to that. I was very much world weary at the time, so it didn't appear to me, to be that much of a sacrifice. Once I had made this sacrifice, I could then settle into my new 'enlightened' life, way up in the far-off yonder hills.

Tradition had it, that it would be required of me to grow a long flowing beard. I would also have to wear rags or a loin cloth, eat only bowls of rice or lentils, and I would have to permanently sever my ties with the rest of humanity, if I was to ever maintain this 'awakened' state of, what I then considered to be, cosmic or supreme consciousness. I would be content – *No* - I really meant to say that I would be *ecstatic* to sit inside my shack or cave, and happily ogle the lacklustre walls all day long. I envisioned that many wandering pilgrims or curious people would surely come and visit me (the peculiar awakened guy up in the hills), and I would dispense wisdom with a free hand. Awakened chaps, I'd heard, didn't take a payment for anything; they were only allowed to live on alms, and whatever passersby placed in their begging bowls.

And so, to my young and embryonic mind, this is how 'I' dimly considered the awakened state and lifestyle to be. Yet this admittedly exaggerated caricature of the awakened lifestyle (or at least a version of it), appears to be lurking at the mental foundation of every spiritual seeker upon this planet. Yes indeed - imagine living out the remainder of your time upon this Earth, with every day 'well spent' cutting yourself off from the life of a world which you are an integral part of. Imagine spending all of your time doing nothing, content to settle for living in squalor, whilst revelling like a junkie in your 'personal' spiritual euphoria all day, every day and for the rest of your life. Now I don't know about you, but the image of that makes me shudder!

False assumptions:

Although the idea of sacrifice and living up in the hills in this manner wasn't 100% appealing to me, I still found that despite this caricatured representation the world held of what it meant to be awakened, the desire for spiritual awakening continued to hold a spellbinding influence over me. I eventually felt that I was _ready_ to do anything at all to attain this state – even yield to this cartoonish kind of lifestyle, if it came to that.

This readiness was further enhanced when I

discovered that many gurus were even promising that with awakening came the ability to work minor miracles, and yet others were guaranteeing the ability to perform *major* miracles, like levitation etc. When I read a spiritual book or listened to a guru speak, I would become somewhat enchanted (hypnotized would be a better word) by what they were saying. It all sounded like it would herald a new dawn of positive change into my life. Then the night would turn to day, the black would change to white, and divine angels would blow their trumpets as the fireworks lit up the darkness, illuminating everything in sight as I 'became' a new Buddha - a new awakened one. However, something which sounded so wonderful also sounded like it would take a super wonderful person to attain it.

Now – I wonder could that possibly be the reason why awakening appears to be such a rare thing in this world? Do we hold awakening at bay ourselves through our beliefs of unworthiness, and our premise that awakening is a super wonderful achievement? Is that the reason why the spiritual search seems to go on indefinitely for many seekers? Perhaps step one on the search for awakening should be a re-evaluation of our belief system, since if we feel unworthy of awakening, then that belief will most definitely hold awakening forever at a distance – like the crock of gold at the end of the rainbow.

Well anyway, due to my belief of unworthiness, I also did what most spiritual seekers do, and

I spent far too many years seeking spiritual awakening. I say 'far too many years', because after a long and unnecessary search, I finally discovered that awakening actually happens in a very ordinary manner. It certainly does not require years of seeking, or battling with those illusive 'inner demons' we all hear about. All this activity of seeking and battling to improve ourselves certainly gives us something to do; it fills up the long hours and keeps us entertained on our path through life. But as far as awakening is concerned, all of that gobbledygook only ever serves to get in awakenings way!

Are you ready for now?

I found that the _readiness_ to allow awakening to occur was a vital ingredient, which had to be in place, before ordinary spiritual experiences could mature into what has been called 'awakening'. One cannot force this readiness, since it is either there or it is not there. I painfully discovered over the years, that most spiritual seekers were really only interested in being _believers_, and in gaining constant entertainment through seeking. Many devoted their lives to a philosophy, a belief system or a 'spiritual' practice, but most 'seekers' had absolutely no readiness at all, to allow an _absolute_ shift within their awareness from dreamland to Reality.

And this is all awakening really amounts to. Once you are totally ready to flow with life as it is, it only requires a mere shift of the attention from the thought world to the *Real* world. There are no beliefs or improvements needed, no battling with sin or past hurts, no divine graces, no trumpets sound and there's no spiritual fireworks either. Like I said, it is quite an ordinary thing, whenever we are willing to see beyond our insistence that it is something which will be forever out of reach and beyond us. It is always readily available, here and now, to anyone who truly desires it. But because the world *believes* that it is like some kind of drug induced high or buzz, we find that many in the world remain as seekers and never finders.

Awakening is not an endless euphoric high. It is also not a fixed and static state; it fluctuates throughout each day. Awakening brings pure clarity, peace, freedom from mental turmoil and awareness of our natural spiritual state in union with life. Various internal spiritual experiences will come and go *naturally*, but one is no longer attached to, or driven by the desire for spiritual experiences any longer. One is then driven by the pure desire for oneness and absolute mental and spiritual freedom!

Awakening arises within the awareness as a response to our willingness, unyielding desire and readiness to allow the present moment to be *just as it is*. There is a sense of surrender which happens when the mind casually gives up its perpetual manipulation and control. This usually occurs when we tire of the stress and effort which mental control brings. If we are always trying to contort our everyday 'reality', or find ourselves making attempts at trying to 'become' a better 'me', then we are not allowing life or Reality to be as it is – we are interfering with life's natural flow.

Awakening happens when we stop battling against our natural self, and when we quit berating ourselves for not being 'spiritual' or 'good' enough. It happens when we stop insisting that we have a troubled past which is torturing us, because the reality is that there is _no past_, until we ourselves bring up a thought of the past in our mind - and even that thought of the past is an illusion.

Awakening happens when we finally understand, that this present moment is the only moment which really matters, it is the only moment that is _real_, and it is the only moment where life in all its fullness takes place. Right here in the _now_ of any and every moment, we can find our freedom from the prison house of thought drama. With every seeming _mundane moment_ we are given an invitation to wake up to the true nature of our Reality. Right here, right now, you too could allow awakening to occur _this moment_, if you were only ready to step outside the mind and embrace life, just as it arises before you, with no more egoic demands being made upon the Reality of now.

How we 'do' this (if it can even be called 'doing') is by shifting our attention out of our thought dramas, and diverting that attention into our senses, to experience real life as it is happening right now. We are then free from the prison of thought, and we emerge fully alive in unity with life/Reality as it is.

Attention to the present is the key to mental and spiritual freedom. If it were not for the many conflicting and confusing teachings which surround the subject of spiritual awakening, many more honest spiritual seekers throughout the world would have awakened with ease, fairly early on in their search.

Yet, although awakening is approached in an ordinary everyday kind of way, its effect can also be at times breath taking. The sense of pure liberation and lack of restriction which arises as a result of the awakening of spiritual awareness, is revolutionary to the sense of the individual 'me', which feels isolated and separate from everyone and everything. Our perception is then transformed with a sense of unity or a blending with all of life. Then a true understanding of the term *'All is One'* finally becomes clear, whereas maybe beforehand it was only an intellectual belief or a theoretical hypothesis.

2
The Thought World

The 'spiritual' thought world:

I have discovered that in the mind of many spiritual seekers, spiritual awakening is perceived to be a difficult thing to allow within ones awareness. However, I have now reached the conclusion that some of those who believe in awakening being difficult, don't really hold this belief due to their lack of understanding, but rather, they believe it simply because they want to believe it. It makes for a good excuse to keep the seeking game going, and tends to lock one into a nice and fluffy little 'spiritual' thought world – a world of belief, a world of philosophy, a world of talk and a world where we seek and do not find.

Indeed, you would find that if you were to *actually* awaken, then it is considered to be politically incorrect to even mention it to anybody. Claiming to be awakened is considered to be an arrogant or an ignorant thing to be doing. Many 'spiritual' teachers are even afraid to admit to being awakened, merely because of this taboo which surrounds those who claim to be awakened. But why do we hold that attitude though?

Some teachers would say that it is because at our centre, there is no-one or no 'me' there to become awakened. So claiming to be awake is then viewed as being rather pointless by some folk. However, this seems like an unnecessary debate to be getting into, since it only makes for more head stuff to trap one within a maze of thought (the thought world). If presently, there is the appearance of an entity in which awakening has occurred, then why deny that by getting caught up in a whole lot of debate over it? This type of debate only fills the mind with confusion, and let's face it, when it comes to spiritual awakening, there is a world of confused teachings out there already. Debates of this nature keep people talking and _thinking_ eternally about awakening, and the end result is usually - no awakening!

Dare I say it, but I feel that the taboos reserved for those who claim to be awakened, are just ego tactics to keep awakening forever mysterious, unusual and at bay, so that the world can remain sound asleep and undisturbed within its dreams of 'spiritual' thought, with no annoying awakened guys pulling back the curtains announcing, _"Waky waky, the night is over and the sun is up, dream time is over. Now is the time to rise and shine!"_

These taboos all keep the 'spiritual' thought world firmly in place. It keeps us all talking, philosophizing, believing and _thinking_ about spiritual matters, without ever awakening out of the 'spiritual' thought world and coming to life in the present Reality of Spirit, as it is exists, here and now.

We should realize that many seekers want to keep seeking and to _never_ find, as strange as it may seem. The 'spiritual' thought world can be thrilling and fun, and whilst we find our 'spiritual' thought world to be thrilling and fun, well then, I guess we just won't find enough desire within ourselves to step out of that 'spiritual' thought world, to embrace the simple wonder of presence.

So, we will find some folks latching onto any old philosophy, belief, debate or excuse at all, just so they can remain asleep in the 'spiritual' thought world. The 'spiritual' thought world is entertaining, and since it's full of beliefs, rules, regulations and long spiritual paths, it makes for a nice pastime or hobby to fill one's life with. Those who treat the teachings of awakening in this manner will always insist upon awakening being difficult, arduous and requiring lengthy spiritual searches.

Now, the reason why most folks like to _believe_ in awakening being difficult, is simply because, unconsciously they know that their manufactured thought identity (ego) would then begin to unravel. After spending a lifetime building up an identity made of thoughts (who we _think_ we are), it could be misperceived that some great sacrifice is being made in order to let that thought based fiction of 'me' go, in order to allow an awakening to the true spiritual nature instead. But it can hardly be considered to be a sacrifice to let go of something as shabby as the ego, in order to awaken to that which is *Real*, such as the Spirit which animates all things. Although, because we have possibly forgotten what being in tune with the Spirit is like, we prefer to think that our 'spiritual' thought world and our dreams of 'me' are far more stimulating than our true spiritual nature.

Well, who would you be without your never-ending daydreams, huh?

The commentator:

The ego doesn't want to let the mind settle down, and it wants to keep at bay what it perceives as being emptiness or 'boredom'. This is why the ego loves philosophy or the 'spiritual' thought world; because this all gives the mind something to latch onto, and it usually generates the false sense of a separate 'me', as one sets about trying to create a new spiritual looking identity to replace what went beforehand.

You see, the ego perceives the peaceful mind as being devoid of any stimulation. Indeed, the ego thinks that peace is *boring*. The ego is constantly interpreting life through thought. It is like having your own personal commentator inside your head, making remarks and telling stories as you go about your day, trying to live your life in 'peace'. Yet all the while, we think that the cause for our lack of peace lies outside of us, but really that cause lies within our own thinking. The inner commentator is always telling us what life is like, and if it is telling us scary, depressing or upsetting stories, then we perceive life to be scary, depressing or upsetting; hence our peace is disturbed. The ego with its commentator is always trying to tell us who we are, what others are like and what life itself is like. Thoughts, thoughts and more thoughts; at all times we have this commentator hypnotizing us with its content. So all that we ever *really* perceive is a thought world, and rarely ever do we experience the *Real* world.

The thought commentator can be very much like one of those television news presenters, who enjoys spicing up a meagre story with a whole lot of lies, just so the viewing public will tune in to hear the 'shocking' news. Nelly Sleepwalker who lives in La La Land will say to her friend, *"Heh, did you hear what the man on the news said; the world's going to hell in a hand basket!"* As Nelly Sleepwalker and her friend believe this 'news', they will find themselves living out their lives based upon it all. Yet all the while they are being fed lies! Just like the news presenter who comments on simple life as if something major is always occurring, the thought commentator in our mind does the very same thing with its never ending thought dramas.

Now imagine if <u>no</u> thought dramas rattled around our mental awareness. What if we began to ignore the inner commentator of thought, and decided to live our lives in a pure perceptual manner, without referring perpetually to the commentator in our heads? Now that's a really *big* question, because we would then have to evaluate just how important or entertaining we find the mental commentator to be. Do we have enough trust in the Spirit to fire the commentator and hire the Spirit instead? Thought dramas and mental strife, appear to the ego as being a means for constant internal entertainment. Most of us like to spin these thought dramas inside our mind for the entertainment they provide, much in the same way as Nelly Sleepwalker likes to obtain her entertainment from watching the 'shocking' news. The ego thrives on these inner thought dramas, even if they cause us to feel like we are living in a nightmare.

So, the ego perceives the relinquishment of its inner thought dramas as being a sacrifice. Without the inner entertainment, it does actually believe that the peace of mind which will ensue is tantamount to a boring stagnation. Of course, one who is lost in egoic consciousness may not realize, that far from being boring and stagnant, the emergence of Spirit within ones awareness, fills one with a sense of abundance, true happiness and authentic peace.

Now, to allow this spiritual awakening to take hold, all we would be 'doing' is diverting our attention away from the internal entertainment and out into Reality instead. When we 'do' this we will be freeing the Spirit, thereby allowing it to flow unencumbered throughout the body and mind. This freeing of the Spirit from the prison of thought would enliven ones perception, mind and everyday life to such an extent, that even the most positive of egoic daydreams would pale in comparison. But there is very little trust on the part of the ego, to believe that the Spirit could do a better job than it does. So we keep our hands gripped firmly upon the steering wheel of our mind, ever fearful to even _dare_ to let go, and surrender to the flow of life instead.

Furthermore, there is a fear which the ego holds, that spiritual awakening brings ego annihilation. Now, this egoic fear is even logically understandable, since the ultimate in spiritual realization, brings about an experience of what can only be termed as being a Void or emptiness. This experience is the ultimate stripping away of all character references, of all sense of 'me', of all individuality and of all everything. This is why I use the word Void, simply because this word describes it closer than any other, but words will never really describe this experience. And the Void experience is just that - an experience. Like all spiritual experiences, it comes and goes; it never hangs around for long, since it would be impossible to operate in that state. However, there is no annihilation as such, but the ego thinks that there is. It is always trying to fill up this perceived emptiness with thought.

With the awakening to your true nature,

comes realization that the psychological 'me' (ego) who we believe ourselves to be, is nothing more than a phantom. In Reality it doesn't even *exist,* and the body will be seen clearly as being a vehicle for the Spirit to play the game of life on Earth. So the fear of the ego (thought identity) to face its own non-existence, and the realization that it is only an appearance in thought, which we have hypnotically given our belief over to, is most intolerable for most folks to even want to hear about, never mind consider – *including most spiritual seekers!*

Where is the willingness?

In truth, the thought identity (ego) which you have been building up all of your life is like a mirage. All that you have ever considered to be 'you' is a lie. Everything you have ever told 'yourself' about yourself – all of your fears and all your little hang-ups are all lies, and have not one bit of truth to them, and never will have!

Everything you say you are and everything you have ever considered to be 'you', was only ever thoughts playing tricks in your mind. Thoughts weaved dreams inside your awareness, and quickly took the throne where your true spiritual nature should be sitting. The Spirit is your Reality and thought identity (ego) is an imposter. It maintains its illusion through mental effort, and acts much like a vampire, sucking on your spiritual energy in order to maintain this deception. Everything it says is 'me' is always changing with no permanence at all, so how can that be real?

This is truly *thee* ultimate realization. For many (including most spiritual seekers) this truth will be rejected, either through fear, lack of trust, or through an un-willingness to let go of the false identity (ego) and its commentating daydreams. Many folk would rather <u>seek</u> and get lost in any sideshow activity which sounds 'spiritual', yet never find the *Real* and simple truth, which is always within them and all around them. These are the ones who would gladly take what the worlds truth speakers have to say, and turn it all into a new religion. Indeed, the best way to stamp down and smother the words of truth in this world, is to either form a cult around it, or to organize a new religion around it. Now, those seekers who actually *are* seeking for the truth of their own Reality, will certainly not be content with organized religions, cults or endless spiritual searches either.

I recall from my own experience, that after ten years of spiritual seeking, I found the search becoming quite a bore. After practicing all of the techniques I had heard about, I found that my mind was still filled with trash thought dramas. I was still somewhat hypnotized by the psychological 'me', and I seemed to be taking one step forward and one step back where spiritual experiences were concerned. I realized that one could spend a lifetime chasing after gurus and having spiritual 'experiences', yet still remain completely asleep and hypnotized by the monkey mind and its fictional character called 'me'. The reason for this is simply because of an _un-willingness,_ to allow the shift of attention from thought to Reality to occur within the awareness. This realization only hit me when I gave up on the search, and got sick of the thought dramas.

However, at the end of all the seeking, a strong desire and _willingness_ grew within me for true spiritual awakening. The thought dramas I held in my mind were starting to tire me out. I was sick of all things that were considered to be 'spiritual', and I found my entire being focused _exclusively_ upon waking up from the thought dreams I had allowed to soil my mind. I then wanted Reality - not experiences, not dreams, not spiritual rules and regulations, not a spiritual persona (new ego) to parade in front of the world; I wanted to get _real,_ quite literally.

The willingness for awakening was then very strong. As I allowed my awareness to remain clear of thought dreams and dramas, I then became gradually aware of my true spiritual nature. I recognized thoughts to be nothing more than merely thoughts, like soap bubbles with no substantiality. Thoughts came and they went, and I found that I no longer had any desire to entertain myself with thought content (daydreams). I understood that I had spent most of my life being hypnotized by the thought content of my own mind.

I found the eventual awakening to be

remarkable, but also very ordinary and quite simple. I realized, that the only reason I believed awakening to be difficult, was because I didn't *really* want to let go of the thought dreams I played with daily. It wasn't until I got sick, sore and tired of the thought dreams that I was finally willing to *allow* them to go. When this willingness was in place, awakening out of those thought dreams was simple. It involved a mere shift of my attention from thought to the present Reality, here and now. An easier way of saying this would be that I came to my *senses*, quite literally!

As some of the gurus had promised, I gradually began to perceive the spiritual truth of others and everything all around me. I realized that I, everyone and everything were the same source playing a game of individuality; playing the game of the psychological 'me'. But although I could perceive this truth in a very un-extraordinary way, I could then also perceive the absolute madness which the psychological 'me' (ego) was composed of. I realized that I had emerged from a mad dream, and I could then see others around me, still very much hypnotized with that dream.

I observed how many people seem to relish this madness with absolutely no desire to ever let it go. I noticed how some spiritual seekers also relish this madness. Everyone seemed to want the dream over the Reality. At first this was somewhat perplexing. This awakening business wasn't at all what I formerly imagined it to be. The gurus didn't tell me, that it would feel much like you were only one of a few awake within a world full of sleepwalkers.

Thought contamination:

So what causes the madness? What causes one to sleepwalk through life? Well, for the average person, their awareness is usually filled with junk thoughts, leaving no room within their awareness for anything else to be realized - never mind the true nature of their own Spirit. Consider that the average person's awareness is like a room, which has been stuffed with a whole lot of old junk. You can barely move in that room, due to the collection of old junk you are hoarding in there. Well the junk in this room is comparable to all of those little thoughts, which are rattling around the average persons mind. When we have our mind filled up with junk thoughts, well then, all we are aware of is the nature of these thoughts. What room will be left in your awareness for the awakening of the Spirit, if you have your awareness saturated in junk thoughts?

A room which has been filled to its capacity with junk, doesn't have any space left in it for anything else but junk, does it? And neither will your awareness have any room left over to be aware of anything else, whilst you have it filled with junk thoughts!

Whilst we have our awareness filled with thoughts, all we will really be aware of is the world according to the nature of these thoughts – hence, we will be living in a thought world and not the Real world. You see, if your awareness is crammed with thoughts all of the time, then what actually happens is that you look out _through_ these thoughts and into the world, thinking to yourself, *"this is the way the world is"*. So all you really get to see, is the world according to the nature of the junk you have lurking inside your mind.

The world is hypnotized with thoughts, which everyone considers to be absolutely true. Through thought we create enemies for ourselves, whenever there may be nobody actually threatening us, or doing us any harm at all. We create belief systems and philosophies, and these contaminate our pure awareness so much, that we dare not even call them into question. We allocate fears and other identifications to ourselves, so we can have a fictional 'me' to parade in front of our friends. But this is all mere thought, and we allow ourselves to become spellbound by it.

Everyone is an actor they say, and this is what you get to see whenever you finally allow awakening to happen. It could be quite startling to observe someone who is putting on an act for you, just because they want you to perceive them as the 'me' whom they like to think they are. It's a bit like being in the twilight zone. Some people like to think of themselves as being the tough guys, or some believe themselves to be shy and introverted, yet others try their damndest to be the centre of attention, but it's all just thought projected out and into the world to say, *"this is me"*.

When we look out into life through this collection of hypnotic thought, we are colouring the world that we perceive. In truth, when we operate from this mode of perception, all we really see is life according to the nature of our thoughts. Therefore, we perceive that which is not *real*, since thought usually interprets life based on what went beforehand (the past). Now, the past is nothing more than a memory trace, which when activated within our mind, obscures the present. Therefore a great deal of the _now_ gets rejected if it is not in line with that which is stored in our memory – in our thoughts. However, if we want to awaken, then we have to look at the root cause which gives us our experience of what we call 'reality'. We are either doing one of two things.

We are either experiencing life directly as it is (pure awareness), or we are experiencing life through the contamination of thought. If we are experiencing life as it is, then we are experiencing _Reality_. If we are experiencing life through thought contamination, then we perceive a delusion. This delusional mode of perception acts much like a fog, which obscures the purity that is our natural state, thereby disallowing us to perceive the natural unity of life as it truly is. Like peering out at life through a frosted window, we can never see clearly. Waking up from this is literally like waking up out of a dream, or shaking heavy smog from our mind. When we allow this to happen, we feel really good since it is a bit like emerging from a haze of fog, out into a clear sunny day, with blue sky and not a cloud around.

So now, taking all of that into consideration; how have you and your world been thus far? Are you at peace? Are you happy or stressed, contented or miserable? What are you looking at life through? Do you see what you _think_, or do you see _what really is_? Are you keeping all of your favourite grievances in mind? Do you persistently relate your victim stories to others? Do you get upset when someone questions your belief system? Are you always reminding yourself and others, of the people you have branded as being your enemies? What movie have you got playing in your mind; a fun loving comedy or a paranoid horror movie? Can you muster up the courage to look within your own mind, and identify what thoughts you are holding there? Can you be brave enough to see the links between your current experience of life, and the thoughts which are giving you that experience?

For example, if you are not at peace, then realize that it is only because you are viewing life through this fog of thought. Peace occurs within a mind which _chooses_ to be at peace within itself. The only thing in this whole wide world which has the power to disturb your natural peace of mind is thought – _your thought_! We may blame everyone else for our lack of peace. We may blame our job or our life circumstances, but a fact which cannot be disputed, even by the most ardent of victim mentalities, is that the thoughts which we hold do indeed contaminate our natural state of peace.

Now, the quickest way to clean up our mind,

is to allow a spiritual awakening to occur within us. Since the spiritual unity of life is the only truth there really is, why would we not allow the truth to be born again within our awareness? It feels a hell of a lot better to live from your truth, rather than to live life whilst gazing at a mental movie. In order for you to come to the realization of that Spirit, you simply have to allow your awareness to clear of what you currently have it filled with. Diverting your attention away from the thought spell and directing it into life as it is, allows your awareness to finally clear. Thoughts will settle down naturally and all on their own, once we stop stirring it all up inside our mind. When we place our *attention* on Reality, then thoughts wither up, since they are not getting the attention they usually get. Just like any old habit in life – when we break the habit, it usually doesn't arise much in our mind anymore. But, I guess it all depends upon what we really want.

So, now can be *your* 'crunch' time, if you so desire it to be. Are you finally ready for now? Half hearted approaches don't work. When we have made our decision definite, then awakening becomes easy. It's like a person on a diet, or like someone who wants to quit smoking. The driving force behind their success is their absolute burning *desire* for the result they hope to attain. So now, what do you *really* desire?

3

The Spiritual Search

The end of the search:

These days there are a growing number of people out there who have spent many years honestly searching for spiritual realization, and they have found their search amounting to nothing but a dead end. They are confused, and they are also frustrated with the many different philosophies and contradictory enlightenment prescriptions available in the world today.

I've come across many who say that they are sick of the continuous search, and claim that they want to mark an end to it all - and this is without even finding that realization which they were initially seeking for. This seems like a pity to me. They have allowed their minds to become so overstuffed with various philosophies and beliefs, they cannot even see, that it is this very accumulation of philosophy and belief which makes awakening *appear* forever distant.

Now, I do indeed understand that a lot of

spiritual seekers are not necessarily seeking Reality or awakening at all, but many prefer to take comfort in their beliefs, rather than be earnest seekers of true Reality. We all know that spirituality (especially new age spirituality) provides a great sideshow of spiritual entertainment, and it is this kind of entertainment which the majority of seekers are really in search of. Inevitably there will be plenty of spiritual sideshow teachers, who will gladly cater for spiritual minded folk who are not really interested in *actual* spiritual awakening, just as there are plenty of actors who will put on a staged performance whenever they have an audience to play to.

However, these are not the kind of seekers I am speaking of here. I am speaking of all those millions of <u>*sincere*</u> people, who actually *do* desire the awakening of the Spirit within their awareness. I am speaking of all those who wish to get *real* once and for all. These are the ones who have most likely put their entire lives on hold in search of awakening.

As a result, they have probably been led a merry dance by various sideshow teachers or spiritual groups. Because of that, they have more than likely become increasingly confused; maybe even more than they were before they began with the spiritual search. In that case, is it any wonder we hear about so many people wanting to call off the search. Although, *eventually* a true seekers inherent sincerity should burst through all of that confusion, as the Spirit within seeks to make its presence known within their awareness.

I fully understand the frustration which sets in as a result of listening to the wrong teachers year after year. However, there are plenty of honest teachers of spiritual awakening out there, and sooner or later (if we are truly sincere) we *will* find someone who will be able to point quite directly at the Reality which we seek, without all of the trappings. We have to keep to it until we find. The frustration alone will help us to spot a truly helper teacher from a sideshow teacher anyway.

There is no doubt that if we are truly and honestly in search of *thee* spiritual Reality, then our search will definitely come to an end someday. But that will be the day on which we will know for certain that we have found what it is we have been seeking for. On that day we may feel like giving ourselves a good slap in the face, for being so asleep that we missed the sheer simplicity of awakening for all of these years. We will then realize that we have spent all of our time and effort seeking Reality like a bird in search of the sky. Now this can be a very weird moment of realization!

I recall the moment when this simplicity struck me. I found myself sitting down shaking my head, almost in disbelief that I had spent so much time, money and effort only to discover that what I was seeking for was truly here and now, already present, within me and all around me, and I just wasn't paying any attention to it. Of course, I had heard the philosophy of it lots of times before that moment, but it never sunk in until I was *finally* ready to let go and embrace the eternal now. In my mind, it all became so simple at that moment. All I had to 'do' was pay attention to life as it was happening all around me. I then chose to experience life fully through my senses, rather than to spend all of my time thinking about it. In all situations I then began to choose life over thought – Reality over the daydream!

My overall desire for awakening finally came forward, and I let go of the mental clutter with _each moment_. Most of this clutter was many of the spiritual philosophies I had satiated my mind with over the years. Now with a new clear seeing, I recognized that much of the philosophy I had once used as a spiritual crutch, was a whole lot of old rubbish – and that is putting it very mildly indeed. To live fully in the moment, I no longer needed philosophy, and I understood that it only ever got in the way anyhow.

You see, no philosophy can contain the truth, because philosophy is derived from thought and belief, and the truth is arrived at by going beyond thought and belief!

Now, because I was interested in what it truly meant to get *real*, I also found myself beginning to let go of a lot of the beliefs I had once cherished, since when we discover the truth, then we also uncover the lies as well. Since my beliefs were constructed from mere thought, I could then _see through_ the spellbinding influence which belief held upon my awareness. Now, this can be a pretty shaky time, if one is not truly sincere about their intention to be 100% free in absolute Reality. I found that my spiritual La La Land was giving way to a state of _Attentive Presence_ through the weight of my desire, and that alone. For without that strong desire to stay clear and attentive to the present, awakening cannot last any longer than a mere momentary experience.

Indeed, even the desire for spiritual experiences should be let go of. Spiritual experiences will certainly come and go more frequently as awakening takes over where the dreams left off, but it is not all about mere experiences. It is about being free in Reality and no longer being captive to hypnotic thought programming. It's about shaking off the spell of thought, realizing our true nature as Spirit in union with the all, and living in absolute clarity and mental freedom!

The search will not end in frustration and then remain at frustration indefinitely. The search ends when we _find_, and if we are indeed sincere about it, then the Spirit will compel us until we _do_ find. We simply cannot say, _"I'm quitting the search"_, because it will not happen that way, no matter how much we like to think we are in charge of this. We will just have no choice in the matter, since it is not the ego which seeks awakening, but the Spirit within us. And when the Spirit has a willing receptacle with which it can bring forth awakening, then the Spirit will eventually have what the Spirit wants!

Spiritual teachers:

Disillusionment with various types of teachers will be the first sign of the search coming to its eventual climax. We will begin to see through the 'mystical' charade which some 'teachers' exhibit. Other spiritual seekers might then call us 'negative' as we call into question the integrity of certain teachers. We may find ourselves cast out into the cold, as we realize that as far as _true_ awakening is concerned, we stand totally on our own - unless we are lucky enough to find someone else with a sincere intent.

This disillusionment phase is not a nice thing to go through. However it is indeed a _necessary_ thing to go through, if we are to ever fully _wise up_. This phase shouldn't last very long though; it all depends upon how daring we are to trust in our own inner guidance. Some might say that it all depends upon how _arrogant_ we are, since paddling your own canoe to awakening can be viewed as being a rather arrogant thing to be doing.

But we should still remain open for any assistance or guidance we may receive, from any _authentic_ teachers we encounter. A true teacher knows the terrain (so to speak). They tend to know all of the pitfalls and all of the snares one might encounter, and they are most likely not afraid to challenge any erroneous beliefs and philosophies we may be carrying. So an authentic teacher can therefore be of great assistance to us (if we are willing to listen to them, that is).

Through the phase of disillusionment, we should be able to recognize a spiritual sideshow teacher from an authentic teacher anyway. We have to watch out when this happens though, because we could become so cynical about misleading teachers that we may end up rejecting the authentic teachers as well. This is called, *'throwing the baby out with the bath water'*. Simple and genuine teachers, can help to make the transition from dreamland to Reality a much smoother ride. So you should accept sensible advice, warnings or good guidance when it comes, and try to keep an open mind - though not *so* open that your brains fall out!

I have been accused at times of being very cynical about some spiritual teachers and their teachings. Well, I have to admit that I am a little cynical about those who would lead <u>*true*</u> innocent seekers upon a merry dance (which usually isn't so merry at the end of the day). Because the merry dance usually takes honest spiritual seekers away off on a tangent, into 'new age' spiritual belief systems (which is like religion in disguise). We can remain forever stuck in those systems if we are not careful.

Some teachers would prefer that to happen though, as they would then get to play the role of the 'guru' indefinitely. If we aren't careful, we could wind up forgetting that our pure intention whenever we had originally set out upon the spiritual search, was for absolute mental freedom and <u>*direct realization*</u> of our true nature as the One (Spirit or God).

Now, saturating your mind with 'new age' philosophy or religious beliefs, has nothing at all to do with Reality and uncovering your *true* nature. Reality has absolutely nothing whatsoever to do with what you think and believe. Dogs, cats and birds don't carry around beliefs, or worry about whether they are treading the right so called spiritual 'path'. Dogs, cats and birds live totally in the present moment without rules, regulations, beliefs, mantras or spiritual taboos. They allow the flow of life or Spirit to move within them freely, activating their natural creature-hood. They are unencumbered by the religiosity we human beings get so entangled by.

What we humans believe is nothing more than thoughts putting on a show in our mind, playing tricks to give us the illusion of security or certainty. Thought has a tendency to hypnotize ones awareness with its content, and if you find yourself gaining comfort from your thought content, then it usually ends up as a set of beliefs.

Now, beliefs may be beneficial when they cause certain effects in your life, like a physical healing or some other such positive manifestation which springs from belief. So it's good to have an understanding of how belief operates, and how thought creates within your everyday experience of 'reality'. However, most of the beliefs we hold can be of an unfavourable nature, and can also be a hindrance to our lives, so why wouldn't we want to look beyond them, to discover something which is *real* and of a genuine and lasting quality?

Our Reality is always there resting patiently; _waiting_ outside the spectrum of thought and belief. Therefore you have to be bold enough to peek out from under your beliefs, in order to live in Reality. I hope that you are brave enough to consider the notion, that spiritual awakening has nothing whatsoever to do with religion, philosophy, belief systems or spiritual rules and regulations.

There's no prayers, incantations, funny sitting positions, mudras, mantras, recitations, hypnotic suggestions, past life regressions or uncomfortable postures required, to gain insight, or acquire firsthand knowledge into your true Reality as the Oneness with the all of life. Awakening is about gaining true freedom and realizing _experientially_ what you truly are. It's about first hand familiarity with your true Reality as Spirit!

Now, the truth is that those seemingly 'innocent' belief systems of the world, have been responsible for much of the world's hatred, fighting, carnage and destruction. _Still_ to this day we can see it going on in the news, with people fighting over religious belief systems. Not until the world awakens from the thought programming (beliefs) it is so spellbound by, will the world awaken to find true and lasting peace.

Being born again:

Really and truly, when we hit upon the end of the spiritual search, it is really only like a beginning. For when the search ends, then the finding should follow soon. It's a bit like being born again, or being renewed into a new life. Even though the outer life may remain the same, everything is as if new, vibrant and injected with life, seen as if for the first time. This is what Jesus meant when he said that we must all be born again. Awakening is a rebirth and a rousing from slumber, as we step out of La La Land and are born again into the *Real* world of Oneness.

Many think that when the spiritual search ends, then that is the conclusion of all the wonder, thrills and adventure which the search sometimes brings. But when the search ends, it is only then at that point, that the *real* adventure can truly begin. At that point when we recognize that we are no longer interested in the merry go round of spiritual seeking, it is then that we may finally allow the awakening within our awareness of Spirit. Then we would find that all of the merriment which the spiritual search has brought us in the past, pales in comparison with this great adventure which awaits us, as we turn away from seeking and move in the direction of finding. For at this point, we will find true wisdom growing steadily within us. We will see things as they really are, and we will be liberated from the maze of thought, and all of the lies we once believed in so deeply.

However, once you recognize that you are no longer caught up in the merry go round of spiritual seeking, and you notice that you are tired of the search, well then, that is when you may drift into a kind of limbo state for a little while. Depending upon your _willingness_ to allow the awakening to occur, this limbo state will be as short or as long as you want it to be. It is like a purgatorial state, lying in wait between seeking and finding, for those who lack 100% readiness to _surrender_ into the now, and be metaphorically born again. During this time you may have all of your spiritual assumptions and beliefs totally destroyed, as you progressively move away from mere belief, towards the desire for what is _Real_.

If you are not 100% ready to align your attention with the present moment, then you run the risk of slipping into a depressive mode, as your false perception of Reality gets untangled and dissolved. It is here that we begin to recognize, that everything which we have believed about ourselves, and all of the meaning we have had in our lives, was held together in our mind like a tapestry made of thought. Really, it's all absolutely nothing but meagre thought! In other words, our whole sense of 'me' is nothing but a psychological conglomeration of thought swirling around our mental awareness, and none of it is _real_ at all. To many folk, the undoing of this mental phantom can be hard to take!

Perhaps most of this undoing will have already occurred as a result of your search, but really, it will only be as difficult or as long, as the strength of your desire to hold onto what is _not real_. Everyone is different when it comes to the willingness of allowing awakening within ourselves. It can be a painful thing to let go of everything we have built up in our mind, which supports and tells the continuous tale of 'me'. But a sincere seeker of the truth will not mind letting go of all that is unreal, in order be born again to the realization of their Spirit and inner truth. They will also not mind letting go of the familiar spiritual search they have become so accustomed to.

Those who hold a strong desire for the realization of truth, will tend to let go of everything that stands against them. Those who are still caught up in the egos materialistic world, seeking for retail therapy, chasing after gurus and other outer things in an attempt to make themselves feel better, generally do not even _want_ to let go of that which is false. These are the type of seekers who want to believe that there are a great many sacrifices to be made, before one can awaken to the Spirit and Reality. They may not realize, that the realization of truth does not require for one to be making any sacrifices at all, except for the relinquishment of the ego.

Now, relinquishing the ego is hardly a sacrifice, because the ego is not _real_, it is only a gathering of thought in our mind. Therefore we cannot say that we are really sacrificing anything at all. The ego is the sole source of all our fears, emptiness, unhappiness, stress and just about every form of delusion we suffer from. Who in their right mind would not want to let go of something which is nothing more than a heavy burden? It is the ego which has us in depression, it is the ego which has us running to therapy, it is the ego which has us addicted to retail therapy, drugs and alcoholism etc.

Dare we let go of this thought made entity, in order to be spiritually born again in truth? When we trade in the ego for the Spirit instead, then we have made the most sensible and profitable transaction we will ever make. Imagine being able to trade in your trash for something which is priceless. Can you even begin to envision what being spiritually born anew would be like? The great release of tension, the feeling of unity, the blending with the all, and the light and care-free outlook on life, really does feel like a completely new start in life.

Now, don't get me wrong here; after awakening you aren't going to be running around with a silly big grin upon your face, buzzing like a cocaine addict. Awakening is really only a simple and casual return to full _sanity_. It's remarkable when it first dawns, but it's still very ordinary and yet strangely familiar. It's much like returning home, where you really always were, but you were just too busy allowing your awareness to be entertained with thought to realize it.

When you do realize that here and now you are all that you'll ever be, and that Reality is _now_ and at no other time, then you can finally allow yourself to rouse from sleep. Then there is crystal clear clarity in all that you see. You are really _there_, 100% alive, maybe for the first time ever. You are looking around you and you see yourself in everything, like you have no edges, like you are space - just empty space. You know that you are nothing, yet everything, and your essence is in everything, yet you also remain as yourself (strange paradox, I know). Words can't really be used to adequately express our truth.

Now, don't misunderstand me, this is still very ordinary and it fluctuates in your awareness throughout the day. So don't be seeking for some static blissful state, because it isn't like that. Yes, there's internal peace, even if you have to deal with a bad situation. Yes, you'll feel happily contented, because you are free of the thought spell, which was the only real source of your discontentment. Yes, you come to know what God is, and that you are one with that very same essence called God. But having said all that, attention to the present moment (Attentive Presence), being the key to this realization, is very, very ordinary indeed.

There's no spiritual qualifications needed for something as simple as that, is there? There's no spiritual search required for you to be as you are, here in the now, presently, fully alive in the moment, is there? Now, why would anyone want to keep awakening at bay, just so they can hold onto the familiarity of a thought made sense of 'me', which is totally unreal anyway? Why would anyone want to repeatedly saturate their awareness with philosophy after philosophy and belief after belief, talking all the time about what it might be like to know the Spirit, whenever they can directly know it for themselves, right here, right now?

4
Liar Liar

The dream weaver:

Now, brace yourself, you may not like what I'm about to say. It has become clear to me that the world is filled to the throat with liars. Of course, I'm not referring to the average type of liar we are all familiar with, like politicians or gossips. The type of liar I'm referring to lives within the mind of everyone on Earth, quite unbeknownst to the majority of humanity of course.

The inner liar (or dream weaver), is the voice in our head which spins that little series of mind movies we play to ourselves all day long. It's almost like our own internal radio chat show. This little dialogue has become something of a substitute for Reality, and it also drowns out the voice of our Spirit, so to speak. Or better put; because we _choose_ to listen to this little mad voice, we cannot hear the voice of our Spirit any longer. It practically leaves our intuition comatose, and the guidance we would receive from that intuition, or

47

inner God, no longer reach's our awareness. This leads us away from going with the flow of life, which is so intrinsic for awakening to have any lasting effect.

Yes, the tendency we have to chitchat and spin daydreams inside our heads makes liars of us all, as we daydream our way into fantasy land, or as I prefer to call it – La La Land. The reason why this liar has lived within the mind almost undetected until now, is very simple to understand. People appear to *enjoy* the lies they tell themselves, and they even more so seem to enjoy the lies they want to *believe* in.

People are always telling themselves lies, as they reconstruct or alter within their mind the so called 'reality' they are faced with daily. We re-run the daily events within our mind, and we overwrite what has happened with what we think should've happened. We do this so that life will appear to fall into line with whatever fantasy we think should be, instead of the Reality of what is. When we alter reality in this mental manner, we tend to feel a little more certain that life is as we *think* it is, even if that perceived life is a living nightmare. However, all the while we are spinning and weaving dreams in our mind, which do not correspond to anything remotely like Reality.

We all like to tell ourselves stories, and we like to *believe* the stories which we tell ourselves, even when they are complete nonsense. Everywhere we go, we meet folk who want to tell us about their altered realities (daydreams) and not about Reality at all. We fill our minds with mental aberrations, delusions and fantasies of who we _think_ we are, and we dream up scary epics of what might be. Then we react to these hallucinations within our mind as if they are real, but all the while we are telling ourselves lies!

I have to endure folk telling me lies all the time. They don't realize they are doing this of course, since as I said, they believe in the lies they are speaking. They tell me things like, _"I am this"_ or _"I am that type of person"_, but they don't appear to realize that the 'I' which they are referring to, is a construct of thought only. These thoughts of _"I am this"_ or _"I am that type of person"_, all arise from memories of experiences which have happened in the past. It is these memories which add the very convincing appearance (illusion) of separate selfhood to the mind. From memory we derive our entire sense of 'me'. We remember who we _think_ we are, based on what went beforehand.

In other words, we _remember_ our entire sense of identity into existence every morning whenever we awaken. So, if we lost our memory, well then, who would we be?

Now, memory is nothing but thought, therefore our whole sense of 'me' is equal to thought, and thought only. The dream weaver (voice of the ego) takes this thought and turns it into stories, which it then tells to itself and also to the world at large. The stories all relate to a 'me' and we become the hero or the victim of our story. But we should realize that this is all a dream - all of it!

We are not our past, or the stories we spin in our heads. We are not heroes or victims; we are pure life energy (Spirit) masquerading as a separate 'somebody' who has a story to tell. This sense of separation leaves us feeling cut off from the absolute true unity of life, and we feel isolated or alone within the great pantomime called 'my life'. The story keeps the psychological construct of 'me' intact, until we are willing to see beyond the thought dramas which hold it in place. The dream weaver is hypnotizing us with its constant internal gibber jabber, with its mental movies and its thought scenarios. That is why people are always telling themselves lies, unknowingly of course.

Now, hopefully this should become clearer to you as we go along, because if it does resonate with you, then maybe you will finally be able to *see through* the little charade your ego has set in place, which distorts your true identity and spiritual awareness.

The psychological 'me':

Most of us mechanically react to every thought which passes through our awareness, as if it were based upon absolute Reality. These thoughts form a pattern in our mind, which then becomes somewhat dreamlike. These dreams tend to saturate our awareness, forming a tapestry weaved of delusional beliefs, psychological fears and phobias, paranoia's, neurosis, inferiorities, superiorities and complexes. These dreams combine, taking a place in our memory, and then they form the hypnotized character I refer to as the psychological 'me' (or ego).

The psychological 'me' is a lie of course, it is made of thought programmes or dreams which we have become hypnotized with. These dreams are all 'unknowing' lies - *we know not what we do'*, so to speak. And as long as we allow the dream weaver to hypnotize us on a daily basis with its daydreams and internal commentary, we never will fully know what we do. Nor will we ever really know our true spiritual nature, due to the dream weaver taking a place in our awareness where the Spirit should be.

Before I awakened from the sleep of hypnotic thought, I couldn't recognize the lies which I told myself. I clung to beliefs and philosophies; mainly for the comfort and sense of certainty they appeared to give me. Anyone who called these mental distortions into question got frowned upon. I built a fortress around my beliefs, simply because they made the world appear more stable, and therefore less chaotic. My beliefs gave me seeming assurances that I knew all about life, death, the meaning of existence and what lay in the 'afterlife'. I was completely wrong of course, since all of this was nothing more than hypnotic thought programming in action. It was a spell of thought I had set in place, to make my life appear more stable. Then, when I allowed my awareness to clear of the thought dramas (lies) I tended to believe in, it became quite startling to observe the lies which others _believed_ about themselves and their lives. It was only then that I realized the extent to which most people have their entire sense of selfhood, derived from hypnotic thought programming (lies).

The source of these thought programmes are obviously built up over the course of a lifetime. But when we _truly desire_ to step outside of this trash and see beyond it all, then these programmes are relinquished fairly easily. Once relinquished or better put, _seen through_, the Spirit comes to the forefront of our awareness, and we then begin to perceive the true spiritual unity of all life. Indeed, when we do finally relinquish these thought dreams, it can be almost funny when you come to observe the trash you once had your mind filled with. You may find yourself shaking your head in disbelief, when you recognize how hypnotized you have been. It is then that you will also stop taking the lies (thought dramas) which others tell you so seriously.

Hypochondriacs are good examples of thought programming. Hypochondriacs have their sense of 'me' derived from imagining that they are sick all the time. They will feed this belief heavily because that is who they think they are - _'Me' the sick person_. In most cases their sickness is not real, but merely thoughts playing a game inside their mind. But most hypochondriacs are attracted to the game thought plays with them; it's familiar to them, and this familiarity strengthens the seeming stability of the psychological 'me'. So therefore, we should not assume that they would want to be 'cured' of their mental malignancy any time soon. If their sense of personhood ('me') comes from being 'the one who is always sick', then if you take that away from them, you would be more or less taking away a large chunk of their thought made identity (ego).

It's the same with some people who seem hell bent on holding onto phobias and the likes. The ego doesn't think that life will be as stable or familiar if it gets relinquished, and when life isn't seen as being stable and familiar, it can be misperceived that life is quite frightening. Exposing the unreality of the psychological 'me' is a scary thing to be doing to a hypochondriac, or indeed, it can be a very frightening thing to a lot of people, who might also obtain a sense of stability from their thought constructed psychological 'me'. This also includes many spiritual seekers, who have their whole sense of 'me' wrapped up in being 'me' the 'spiritual' person.

I recall hearing one of my local doctors complain once, that almost 85% of his time was taken up with hypochondriacs. He said that he was seriously considering giving up the whole doctor thing, because he was so sick of them. No matter how often he told them that there was nothing wrong with them, they would argue that there was something wrong. Some of these hypochondriacs would even fall out with him, and then go visiting *another* doctor until they got the 'verdict' they desired – until someone else agreed with the _lies_ they believed in about who they are. It is important to the hypochondriac that others view them in the way they see themselves, because if it was proven that they are not what they think they are, then what are they? They would feel completely lost without that seemingly 'stable' sense of 'me'.

Perhaps you know of someone who likes to tell you fairy stories about their life, or about who they like to think they are. Maybe they are not a hypochondriac but something similar; like a paranoid person who believes that the world is conspiring against them, or someone who thinks they are 'king of the hill', or maybe just someone who believes that they have a phobia. You should try telling them that what they _believe_ isn't true at all, but is just a few thoughts rattling around inside their mind which they have hypnotized themselves with. Tell them that they *"know not what they do"*, as Jesus is reported as saying. And then prepare to take your guard, as you behold the irritation growing within them right before your eyes.

It can be quite shocking, seeing some of the reactions you will get from pointing out the truth. You see, you will be messing with their _altered_ reality and pulling at their sense of 'me'. If there is one thing I have come to understand the hard way, it's this simple fact - folk don't like having their altered realities or thought made psychological 'me' messed with, at least not until it causes their life to become extremely boring, or until it turns their life into a living hell.

Fear of the Void:

After I finally allowed the awakening to Reality within my awareness, I could then see clearly that the majority of humanity (some more so than others), really believed the stories they filled their minds with. It became quite clear to me, that the egos whole sense of 'me' was nothing more than a delusion to replace our true identity as Spirit (the God within). When I was a spiritual seeker, I read all about the ego being a delusion, but I never really understood it until I let go of my own delusions.

These stories we fill our minds with tend to maintain an illusion of control. If our view of life and the world seems predictable and controllable, then life doesn't seem to be such a scary business, does it? Well, when we think we know what is going to happen tomorrow-week or tomorrow-month, well then, that's manageable isn't it? We then *think* we have life by the short and curlys. We dream that we are in the driving seat, firmly with our hands upon the steering wheel of life's flowing current, don't we?

Then again, maybe we tell ourselves stories just to relieve some of the boredom we might be feeling. Yes, we all know how those little thought dramas inside our minds, are every bit as entertaining as the dramas we see on the television. Indeed, anything will do as long as it fills up the emptiness, as long as it fills up the Void we unconsciously fear is there lurking at our centre. We unconsciously know this Void is there, and because we fear that it is a vacuum of nothingness, we do all that we can to avoid it, including telling ourselves depressing or scary stories.

Yes, we will try to 'become' anything in order to avoid the emptiness we fear we are immersed in. We will even try to become spiritual seekers in order to avoid it. But we are not really seeking the Spirit, are we? What we are seeking for is the substitute for true spiritual realization. What we are seeking for is a spiritual sideshow to entertain ourselves with, aren't we? We are seeking to create a new psychological spiritual 'me'. But in doing this, we are trying to strike a bargain with the inner God, so that we can hold onto our delusions and only pay lip service to the truth, by turning it all into another philosophy. Our fear of what we think is Void and empty is the reason why the _true_ truth speakers have always been burned at the stake, crucified, slandered and abused. It is perceived that the true truth speakers are a danger and a threat to all that is 'me', even for the spiritual version of 'me' which many weave for themselves these days.

Yes, the egos world will stamp out the truth with its falsifications at all times, to keep at bay what it perceives as being the emptiness of the Void, which it unconsciously knows is the _ultimate_ true nature of Reality. These falsifications will usually emanate from teachers of the common and accepted ways. Now, the common way used to be organized religion, but is now the way of eastern methods. Seekers think they are being rather modern by leaving behind organized religion and taking up some eastern practice, but all that usually happens is that they swap one belief system for another.

Could this be an ego attempt of striking a compromise with the Spirit like, *"Let's settle for a new type of religion or a philosophy, instead of awakening?"*

Yet all of this philosophy and organized effort, only ever serves to stand in the way of the *true* seekers of truth. The totality of life cannot be stuffed into the tiny box of our philosophies and religions. Spirit/God transcends all of our tiny ideas and belief systems. Reality truly is Void or empty of such thought contamination.

We fear that the Void is pure emptiness, like we will be floating in a big black nothingness if we surrender to the flowing ebb of Life. There is a mental image which comes from ego, that the realization of Spirit involves a blanked out state, where we will be in some kind of weird empty permanent trance with a nothingness of all sensation. We unconsciously fear that we will be left with a joyless, dry and arid mode of being, where no life or anything resides. This is what the ego would have us believe anyway. But you have to understand that the opposite is the case.

This Void cannot be strictly called emptiness; it is actually pure *fullness*. It is the pinnacle of all life, the climax which humanity and all life forms strive for. It is that which gives life to all that we perceive, and all that we are.

The animals are that, the ocean is that, the air is that, the Earth is that, your greatest enemy is that and so also is your best friend that. This Void is God, and it is *you* - This is our absolute Truth!

But we still fear our spiritual truth, and we prefer to spin stories within our mind as a replacement for our true being. The stories could relate to anything at all, as long as it is *not* the truth. This is when the psychological 'me' (thought identity or ego) comes in handy. The psychological 'me', being nothing more than a collection of thought, will always try to take the place of our true identity as Spirit/God, the absolute fullness that is the Void.

Altering Reality:

At the very moment you open your eyes in the morning, you immediately begin to tell yourself lies. For in those first few 'waking' moments of each new day, you construct within your mind all of what you *think* you are, and all of how you perceive the world to be. Maybe you *remind* yourself that you are a stressed person, or that the world is a terrible place. Maybe you bring to mind that you are an unhappy or neurotic person. Maybe you tell yourself that life is tough; *"It's a rat race out there, it's kill or be killed!"* The possible combinations for lies are endless.

Lie upon lie you construct an altered reality within your mind. And _altering_ Reality is exactly what you are doing every morning. With thought you create a make believe world inside your mind before you even get out of bed. You look out into life through this make believe thought world, and all you ever see is your lies. Your make believe is spread out over the world tainting everything you come upon; from your own self image, to your perception of others, to the world as you perceive it to be.

Now, what would it be like if you just woke up one morning, and allowed your mind to remain clear? What if you didn't bother to re-run all of those little _reminders_ of what you are, what others are and what the world is like? Yes, I wonder what life would be like then, huh? Indeed, in those few 'waking' moments after your night-time sleep ends, many thoughts roll together in your mind to remind you of how the world is, and to remind you of who and what you are. For in those few moments you formulate your world view, and all of those beliefs of 'me' – and so does everyone else, and this is the reason why I say that the world is full of liars.

You think you know who and what you are. You tell yourself your story of 'me' every morning, and then you go out to meet the world, so that you can tell everyone else you meet all the stories of 'me'. As you tell the stories of your 'great' adventures, of what you did and what you said, piece by little piece you attempt to convince the world and yourself, that you are what you _think_ you are. If enough of the world agrees that you are the semblance of this story called 'you', then it is copper fastened, isn't it? Well at least it is within _your_ mind anyway.

Here in your little dream of 'me' where the storyline hardly ever changes, you try to maintain a tightly held grip upon yourself and your life. You try to steer the wheel of your life, in accordance with all of what you think you are. When you are invited to consider something new, to consider the possibility that you may not be what you think you are, then you might say, "_Oh no, I'm not interested in that kind of thing._"

You keep telling yourself that you are the great one, the inferior one, the neurotic or the hero. You tell yourself that you are Fred, Sally, Bob or Nicola. You are a dentist, doctor, window cleaner or shop keeper. You think you have phobias and emotional 'issues' which need working out – on and on it goes. All of this stuff hypnotizes your awareness with lies and with a thought made character which turns you into a puppet, which is being dangled by the strings of thought. Yes indeed, your altered reality begins to take shape at the very moment your night time sleep ends - and it is this state of affairs which we have come to call the 'waking' state!

The people of the world apparently 'wake' up from their sleep each morning, but really what is happening is that they are drifting from one stage of sleep into another stage of sleep. But sleeping is nice isn't it? You are there lying in your pit, all comfortable and dozy; maybe you are having a 'nice' little fluffy dream. Do you really want to wake up from the *familiarity* of the dreams you are spinning within your mind?

Now understand this - Your altered reality called 'me' is a lie; it has nothing to do with Reality. You may enjoy your lies but you will never make them true, not even to yourself, because there might come a day when the lies just won't do it for you anymore. Life has a way of crushing the fantasies of dreamers, so that the Spirit and Reality can be allowed to take hold of the reigns. You may tolerate the struggle of grasping the reigns of life's chariot, of turbulently fighting against life's flow, but the stress of it all will eventually show up, and if you don't surrender to the flow of Life (Spirit), then that stress will wear you down, until maybe there is a breaking point. You might be a glutton for punishment. Maybe you even receive your daily entertainment from stress, struggle and strife, but know this and know this fully – Spirit does not sustain that which fights against the flow of Spirit! Hence, this is why people have nervous breakdowns, depressions and panic attacks; it's why they get run down with stress disorders and the likes.

So now, how much do you really want to stand face to face, with the unadorned truth of your Reality?

You know, there will be no *lasting* realization of your truth, until you are willing to see through all of your lies. You may have momentary glimpses of truth, but awakening to your true Reality is not about momentary glimpses, it is about an abiding realization with lasting effect. That is not to say that it is like some kind of weird super duper unending buzz, like you have popped an illegal pill and then you are permanently high, mystically charged with super powers. It is merely about recognizing the lies as lies, and choosing Reality instead. _The lies are just thoughts_, so in any moment of time you have the choice of either joining your attention with thoughts or Reality. By making this choice, you should easily see through all of the lies you have been cherishing.

Is it easy to see through the lies? Yes it is; but how do you see through the lies? Well, you've got to realize that the voice in your mind is telling you lies to begin with, and then you have to be brave enough to admit that fact to yourself.

Come on now, be brave!

Inside your mind, you like to tell yourself that the world is just the way you _think_ it is. Then you spread those lies to others; trying to gain allies to support your view of yourself and the world. And when someone else supports your view of things, well then you tend to 'like' that person. But if they don't support your view of things, well then you don't like that person anymore.

Many prefer to believe in the psychological 'me' (ego) as being who they are, for fear that the ground will open up and the Void will swallow them whole. They don't want the truth of who they are, they only want the lie (the ego) because it is familiar to them. They will always try to alter Reality according to their known past, so that life appears stable and predictable – so tomorrow will always be the same as yesterday.

Now, which one do you see yourself as? Do you see yourself as being the one who wants the truth, or as the one who wishes to be a sleepwalker? Can you stomach the truth? As some poor lost soul once said to me, *"Look, I know it's the truth, but I just don't want to hear about it!"*

Yes, all of those little hang-ups, the inferiorities and superiorities; all of those little inner lies (thoughts) have to be seen for the _mirage_ which they truly are, if you want Reality to take hold. But who would you be without all of that trash cluttering up your mind? Yes indeed, who would you be? I can tell you for sure, that who you would be, is what you *really* are. You would be trading your limited thought identity (ego), for realization of your inner abundant truth and Reality; that truth and Reality being _God_ of course!

5
Behold Reality

What should we do?

Some gurus tell us that we have to 'do' this or 'do' that, in order to realize the true nature of our Reality. This of course gives rise to effort. But surely there is no actual 'doing' required to merely shift our attention into Reality, thereby bringing our spiritual truth into awareness. Obviously we have to 'do' something to cover up or distort our awareness of what is real, do we not? Surely we must be already constantly 'doing' something within our awareness, which makes us all unrealized when it comes to awareness of our truth and Reality. So then, what are we doing to block out awareness of our Reality? Have a look within your mind and you should have no problems in answering that question. Where is your attention? Are you being attentive to Reality (the present moment) at all, or are you lost within the dreamland you carry around inside your head?

In order to be _aware_ of anything, then we have to give our _attention_ over to whatever it is that we wish to be aware of. So it is the same with spiritual realization, awakening or pure awareness; whatever name you want to give it. To bring realization of our Reality into awareness, then we have to give our attention over to what is _Real_, and we have to divert our attention away from what is un-real. The awareness is always there and the Spirit is always there; it's just that we are constantly drowning our attention in a sea of thought, so we tend to live our lives unaware of our true nature.

Does it not make sense that we fully perceive, only what we place our attention upon? So now, what are we placing our attention upon? Have we got our attention on _Reality_, or on some other altered 'reality' which we are dreaming up in our mind? What is taking the throne in our awareness; Reality or a daydream? Since no real 'doing' can possibly be required to be in alignment with our inner truth, then awareness of that truth cannot possibly be a difficult, or a hard thing to be aware of. Surely no spiritual search is required to find that which is here and now; that which is real? What effort or exertion could really be required, in being true to our natural selves, and in being true concerning the expression of that natural self within the world? Exertion lye's only in fighting against the natural self, not with being in alignment with it.

We are contaminated with the viewpoint that

we are some lowly species, unfit for the realization of our natural state - the Spirit of God which lies within everything. We unwittingly operate on automatic pilot, dreamily infecting our minds with heavy leaden thoughts which are at variance with this natural state of pure Spirit within. Because we have handed over every aspect of our mental attention to running these thoughts in our mind, we leave no space within our awareness for anything else but thought.

We may then feel that we have to fight our way out of these thoughts, to ever discover our true nature. So we practice mental disciplines and meditation techniques, breathing exercises, Tai Chi, Yoga and chakra balancing etc. We might do all of these things because of an underlying belief that awareness of the true nature of our Reality is a difficult thing to accomplish, and so consequently requires a lot of effort and practice. And then there are plenty of 'teachers' out there, who will gladly assist our belief in awakening being a difficult thing to accomplish.

So, we listen to our teacher and he gives us a philosophy. Now, the philosophy is meant to help us awaken to the truth of our inner being, but usually all it ever does, is to further hypnotize our mind with even more thought. We might end up talking the talk alright, but as far as an awakening is concerned, we more often than not, don't get to be awakened. We usually settle for _believing_ in whatever the guru is saying, rather than bringing to life within our own awareness, the spiritual Reality which the guru is speaking of.

We may also find a belief growing within our mind that we are lacking in some manner, and so we may declare ourselves inadequate or unsuitable for spiritual awakening. But we are not unsuitable, unfit or inadequate by any means, since it is only our chaotic heavy thinking which is defective. Only these disordered thinking patterns, manifest that which appears as 'bad' within us and within our world. When we mistakenly perceive our thoughts as being what we are, then it surely can seem to be true that we are a low life species. But seen from the perspective of spiritual awakening, we are *very* far from low. When these heavy and dead thought patterns are shaken off, we then realize that which we truly are, and we then see everything around us as it truly is. It is then that we will honestly declare to the world, that all is pleasant and *all is well!*

In order to come upon that realization of truth, we do not require any effort or 'doing' at all. We actually need to *cease* our minds incessant and never ending doing. We need to leave behind our constant *doing* in constructing the La La Land of daydreams, which tire our mind and body. We need to shift our attention to the *Real* and away from the un-real. Many sincere seekers misunderstand this 'do nothing' talk we hear from various teachers. They will take it quite literally, and then end up with a mind full of second hand philosophy, and as a result, they may forever remain un-awakened. Yet all that is required for the realization of our truth and

Reality is this small shift in our attention, away from that hypnotic trance of thought which we hold so dear, and into our _senses_, diverting our attention back into life/Reality; the here and now, just as it is!

Is it any wonder people get confused by this. They are told to 'do nothing' by many teachers, and they don't fully grasp that by shifting their attention to the _Real_, then that is actually how the mind ceases its constant and never ending doing. Now a shift of attention cannot in any way be considered, to be an act of 'doing'. We do not have to 'do' something in order to shift our attention from one thing to another. A shift of attention is not a strenuous art form, which requires lots of practice. It only takes an honest willingness for it to happen, and obviously, we have to fully _want_ the awakening to happen also. Many people say that they do want to awaken, but when you really listen to them and the many excuses they make to remain asleep, you will find that they don't _really_ want to awaken. And why is that? Well, because there is no trust that the Spirit will make things better for them.

There is a deep fear of letting go of the control which the ego exerts. Now, we should all realize that awakening does require this _trust_, that the Spirit will enliven our being far more than we could ever _think_ possible. The trust required, is similar to that trust you would need just before making a bungee jump. Awakening is exactly like a bungee jump into unknowingness, or into the Void of our being. We have to trust that we are being held securely, and that we won't falter through allowing the awakening of spiritual awareness.

We are afraid to let go fully, because we tend to think that through the thought content of our mind, we can give our lives some meaning, but our lives will never have any true meaning until we awaken to our inner truth. The 'meaning' which thought appears to give our lives, is always very short lived. When our egoic 'meaning' fizzles out, we usually end up wondering where all of the magic went to, as we lament the past and yearn for it to return to us. The ego mind teases us with this mental nonsense, and that's why most of the world remains stuck in their past. Most folk get to a certain age, and then they are always found to be telling the tales of yesteryear, whilst believing that the good times have past them by, and now all they have to look forward to is getting older – merely existing from day to day, and no longer really *living* life with passion.

This need not be the case though. This is the way the ego lives, but the awakened live in a very different manner. The awakened are free from the egos boring tiny world, they are free from its dictates, its system of conformity, its rules and regulations and its constant rehashing of the past. If we truly seek for this kind of freedom, then we need to trust in our Spirit, and let go of the steering wheel of our life. We need to jump into Reality, just like a free fall, and we need to enjoy the ride, because it certainly is a whirlwind adventure!

The spiritual stereotype:

There really is no effort required in this whole business of awakening. When we have had our gut full of the ego mind and its thought spell, then awakening is the easiest thing in the whole wide world. It's like a tipping of the scales, where more weight finally shifts over to the awakening side of the scales, than there was on the sleeping side. But if on some level we don't actually *want* to let go of our thought dreams, then we may try to convince ourselves and our teacher that awakening is indeed a difficult thing. But you know, it is only ourselves we will be fooling, and only our own time and money we will be wasting, as we run around buying numerous books and visiting various teachers. Those who are ready for awakening will awaken, and those who want to remain asleep will stay asleep, despite declaring themselves to be 'spiritual seekers'.

They aren't really spiritual seekers at all; what they are is entertainment seekers. Listening to the guru becomes exactly like watching an interesting movie on the television. They listen to the gurus' words and then turn what he has said into a set of beliefs (like hypnosis). No harm in that I suppose, it could make for a nice little dream. It's a pity though; being exposed to the teachings of truth and then ignoring it all, simply because you are treating the teacher like he is some sort of stand up spiritual entertainer.

The spiritual seeker, who wants to stay in the thought dream, usually settles for getting involved in a whole lot of effort; what has become known as the effort of becoming. It's like a game we might play with ourselves. Really it's the old performance of trying to sound like, look like, and act out the behaviour patterns of what we think a spiritual person should behave like. The spiritual stereotype is what I call it. This never leads to awakening though, even if we somehow manage to fight tooth and nail against our true nature, and to some extent manage to keep this so called 'spiritual' act going 24 hours a day. This performance is just another way of trying to alter our personality, so that we can be accepted – maybe this time by God. It operates as a major blockage to discovering the truth within, since this performance is not in line with truth. This is a lie which we are persistently upholding, and lies act like clouds which obscure the sunlight of truth.

To be aware of the Spirit, we do not need to run around like some spiritual stereotype saintly figure, with a make-shift halo floating above our heads - most certainly not, because that would not be _real_. Many honest spiritual seekers get caught up in the effort of trying to become this stereotype mockery of what we _think_ spiritual is. But trying to become something other than what we actually are is once again, interfering with our Spirits true natural expression. Now, the Spirit will never express itself in a bad way, only thought will do that. Spiritual stereotypes are the produce of thought, they come from sources which we gather from outside of our true being; usually from laws and rules conjured up by a religion, or possibly an egoic 'spiritual' teacher. But don't you see that the truth is not a lie – *it is a truth!*

Trying to force ourselves to fit into someone else's' picture of how we should be behaving is restricting, and it requires for us to operate a major censor within ourselves. Now restriction and censorship are not ingredients which give rise to the birth of spiritual freedom – most certainly not. Freedom comes only when we <u>*see clearly*</u> the hypnotic grasp which thought holds upon our awareness, and we then recognize thought for the illusion that it is, and as a result of that clear seeing, we decide to move beyond thought and into Reality instead. So restriction and censorship give birth only to <u>*slavery*</u> and not freedom. Therefore trying to mould our behaviour, in an effort to put on the performance of the spiritual stereotype, or to 'become' what a religion or a guru says is 'spiritual', is exactly like a willing slavery. This takes an awful lot of energy, and it stands as a major blockage before the truth within.

But heh, this effort of becoming, at least it can become our new hobby, since it keeps us busy with a forever task, which we will never ever fully master. It reminds me of playing Golf. Golf is a game even the best say you can never fully master, but many will still die trying, rather than just giving up and enjoying the game, *as it is!* So, trying to become something that you are not, will never win out at the end of the day either;

it'll just stress you out and ruin your enjoyment of life. But as we all know, some like the stress game, even if it ruins their enjoyment of life. So, the effort of becoming is an interesting little game we can play to try altering our true self, so we can 'become' what we think we should 'become'.

I have a question for you. Spend some time considering the ramifications of this question as it relates to your identity. Ask yourself now, and wait for an answer - *Am I, what I think I am?*

Spiritual awakening is nothing more than a clear seeing of all that we are not, and a direct realization of what we truly are. It is a clear seeing of life as it is. It is a pure awareness that we are <u>One</u> thing appearing as everything. We are that pure energy, Spirit or consciousness which gives birth to our life, world and universe. Thought borrows energy from this pure source to create a substitute for our true nature. From memories based upon past conditioning and life events, we automatically create 'me' as we drift along through life. We gather learning's, enemies, friends, neurosis and addictions etc. All of these things become habits which get ingrained into our awareness. When someone says to us, "*so tell me about yourself*", we usually recite from this list of memories saying, "*this is me*".

Because of the egos hypnotic effect upon our awareness, it puts up an extremely convincing illusion. Most of us never consider the possibility that this thought made version of 'me', is a complete hallucination. Our story of what we call 'me' is part of a memory trace. It is like a computer program which we are constantly updating. But all of this is just thought rattling around inside our head. This is what we use to meet the world with.

We do indeed have a uniquely programmed natural genetic character to play the game of life with, but because our natural genetic character maybe isn't in line with the silly stereotypes of the world, we begin to feel like something isn't right with 'me'. So we begin to act out the part of how we think we should be, lest someone criticises us or makes fun out of us.

So we take to spirituality, which on an unconscious level holds the belief that we are not worthy enough for the promise of spiritual awakening. We embrace that unconscious belief, and once again get caught up in the egos world of becoming. We usually end up suffocating our natural self as we fight to become, become and become. And all the while whilst we are doing this, we are putting up invisible barriers to awareness of our true natural self.

Now, if we could only *cease* this endless cycle of becoming, by embracing who and what we naturally are - not what we think we are, or what we think we have to be – then ease, peace and the flowing river of life will reveal itself, to smooth our way in this world. The way will then be left open finally, for *true* spiritual awakening to occur.

Attentive Presence:

Now, attention to the present moment is the key to spiritual awakening; I simply call it _Attentive Presence_. With Attentive Presence we become simple minded, not docile or stupid; it's just that our mind becomes clear and free from the burden of fixed thought patterns and we become simple, living life in the moment. Some have tried to turn this into a technique but it is not a technique, since children are mainly living in this mode quite naturally, as we too once were (perhaps you remember it).

However, as we grow older and the world closes in around us, it usually leaves us with a mode of being where we end up _thinking_ more about life, rather than truly _living_ life in the present moment. Therefore the present moment usually eludes us, as we spend our time thinking, thinking and thinking. Attentive Presence brings an end to the thought spell, and leaves us awakened to our true spiritual nature, free in life and in spiritual union.

A rolling stone gathers no moss they say. Well, with Attentive Presence you will no longer gather any moss (thought dramas) within your mind, and no moss of thought shall stick to your awareness any longer. You'll be free to flow through life, fully enjoying your true natural character. No longer will the effort of becoming taunt you. Once you know that you fully desire awakening, and realize that you are indeed worthy of it; when you trust that the Spirit can brighten your life better than the psychological 'me' (ego) could ever do – then you can finally make that *definite* decision to awaken, and live your life with Attentive Presence, in Reality.

Now, the following guidelines for Attentive Presence are taken directly from my first book *'Finding Reality'*. If you have already read this book then you might want to re-cap, or else just move onto the next chapter.

From 'Finding Reality'

Now, let's define *Attentive Presence* a little clearer, since it is *Attentive Presence* which allows for awakening to occur. Let's get a little technical here just for a moment. Throughout my years as being a spiritual investigator, it used to irritate me greatly whenever I heard teachers talk about being in the present moment. Why did I get irritated? Well because they would leave you high and dry, and never go into the particulars of how one was actually supposed to join their attention with the present moment.

They would of course blather on about how it was not something one could '*do*', and that we have no choice as to whether it happened or not, because there is '*no-one*' there to make a choice. Of course, this made me want to *yawn, yawn and yawn!* Hence I always found myself getting mildly irritated with all of this babbling guru speak. Yet, maybe I'm stupid, but I have never understood a mere shifting of attention as being an act of '*doing*'. Nevertheless - *codswallop aside*

- what follows is the simplicity of shifting your attention away from thought dreams and dramas, into Reality instead, in a way that possibly a child could understand.

Come to your senses!

You've heard that before, haven't you? There's nothing new here for you then, is there? Or could you possibly believe that this is far too simple to be effective, for awakening to Spiritual Reality? Well, who said life had to be complicated anyway, perhaps life is simple after all? Anyway, let's go into that a little deeper, just incase you are bewildered by what *'coming to your senses'* actually means.

In order to be Attentive to the present Spiritual Reality, then we have to realize that the spiritual Reality we are seeking for is here and now, within us and all around us. So, we have to perceive that Reality in the only way that we can perceive, and that is through each of our five senses. If we shift our attention *fully* to whatever we experience here and now, in each of our senses, then our mental awareness has not got any room left over to be sleeping in the *La La Land* of thought dreams – thus we shake off the dreamland and wake up to Reality!

If we are doing anything at all, for example, driving the car, working, reading, washing up, playing sports, gardening, walking, listening or talking, eating, watching the T.V (in short, anything), then keep your full attention in your senses - *without the inner thought commentary!*

This is pure experiencing, and it allows for us to encounter an uncluttered, wakeful and alert pure awareness. Start with what you hear, then maybe move on to what you feel, see, smell, taste – go around your senses drinking in all that life has on offer, getting out of your head and being fully *Attentive* to the *Present moment.*

Then when ones awareness is kept clear of the thought traffic, one begins to perceive Reality through the eyes of the Spirit. This is when we will stumble upon the present Spiritual Reality we have been ignoring, possibly for all of our lives. However, we should make no demands on what we *think* we should experience; we simply kick back, united with life as it is, savouring and appreciating like a connoisseur, the moment that is now.

Thoughts will still come and go, but this is what we should *allow* them to do – *to come and go* – we certainly should not allow ourselves to get caught up in any daydream scenarios or thought dramas. We simply wake our attention up out of its sleep, and allow ourselves to become *attentive to life as it is* - to let our attention *bypass* any daydreams or thought dramas that may be running in our mind. Soon we will find that the hypnotic spell of thought (*La La Land*) is broken, and our attention is awakened with the new wakeful momentum of *Attentive Presence* instead – hence the popular word spiritual seekers use – *Awakening!*

6
Dialogues

Q: What is the point in us having a body, work, children or relationships, if it is only the inner spiritual nature that matters?

A: The reason why the inner spiritual nature matters the most, is because what we have going on within us, is what we experience as our world or 'my life'. We will always experience life in accordance with what is going on within our mind; therefore it is imperative that we keep our inner mental space healthy, clean and clear.

We are either projecting thought or seeing what's real. Therefore if we keep our awareness clear of unreal thought scenarios, we get to see what's real and are no longer experiencing a world of make believe, or a world of fear, malice and hatred etc. We experience the world as it truly is, because we are operating from our inner truth and no longer from thoughts dreamed up in our mind.

As for the point in work, children or relationships; well these things will still go on, and as a result of approaching these things with awareness of what's real, we will enjoy them more fully. We then approach everything (work included) with an unattached frame of mind. Awakening releases us to experience life in a care free manner.

Don't forget that the One (Spirit/God) is not only within us, it is also within the apparent 'others' we see. When we are in touch with our own inner truth, we perceive the inner truth of others also. We will no longer _react_ so much to what we think of others, since we will know the truth instead. But don't me wrong, this also doesn't mean that we are going to like the mindset of everyone we meet. Once awakened, we may find that we no longer have any desire to share company with certain people, simply because we will no longer be on the same wave length as them. We may know the truth, but we are also going to be faced with the conditioned mindset of others also. If someone is heavily steeped in egoic consciousness, then we won't have much in common with them, even though we will still recognize that we are all made of the same 'stuff'.

Q: Sometimes I feel that if I could only get away from the busy world, then awakening would be made easier.

A: I understand what you mean. Sometimes it

can feel like that, but try to realize that we don't need to give up everyday life for awakening to occur; this has been a misunderstanding within the world for millennia. That's why many people went to live like hermits. They felt that they needed to give up worldly life to awaken to their inner truth. They also felt that they had to deny the body any sort of physical comfort. The body is part of our experience in this world; if the Spirit didn't want this experience then it wouldn't happen. So the Spirit clearly wants to engage in, and fully enjoy the whole 'life on planet Earth' scenario.

Once awakened, I found that I didn't need to give up this, or deny that. I only had to stay clear enough for the truth to come alive within my awareness. When that awakening happened, I found that I actually embraced life more fully, since I made no more demands upon it. I could let life be as it is, leaving me to accept each and every moment just as it is, without prejudice, stress, hatred, fear, greed or any of the many mental afflictions associated with the egoic 'me' and its thought spell.

Q: How do we know that the only thing which is real is the Spirit we have within us?

A: Actually the Real is not only within us, it is within us and all around us. It pervades everything; the world and the universe. We are the same source manifesting as that everything. The same source (which is our true nature) beats our heart, makes the wind move, causes the planets to travel around the sun and keeps the sun itself burning. Awakening involves the realization that I am the all - I am the One!

Reality at its most subtle is a unified field of energy, from which we derive our being. The scientists who study quantum physics know this now as a fact. Some scientists call this field the Zero Point field. They know it holds a source of immense power. It has been called by many names. It has been called the Tao, Nirvana, the Kingdom of Heaven or simply God. We could go on with the names and labels ascribed to it, but the realization in awareness is the important thing. When that realization hits home, then we understand that we *are* that unified field of energy, _we are that_, we are not apart or separate from it, and we do not have to join with it either, since we already are united with it. Only experiential realization of this is what is required.

Once we have this realization, we will no longer be totally fooled by appearances, nor will our thoughts seem as serious and substantial as they once appeared to be. You see, we usually accept every thought we have as being a correct interpretation of reality, but thought contaminates reality, it does not actually interpret reality correctly at all. Therefore a thought based, or a better way to put it would be, a thought generated reality, is not Reality at all in the strictest sense, since it is based upon make believe (what we think). Pure awareness is devoid of all interpretations (positive or negative) and demands or alterations made upon the moment of Reality's now. Therefore the *Real* can only be experienced in awareness when we let go of the un-real from our awareness. Now - thought is the un-real!

Q: But surely we need thought?

A: We don't need it as much as you would suppose. Have you noticed that most of our good ideas just seem to come from nowhere – right out of the blue, usually at a time when our mind is quiet? We certainly don't need dopey daydreams running in our mind all day either. Thought is a tool of creation, we can use it to shape and mould pure source energy, to create within the world we see around us (as we perceive it to be).

Now, our current problem is that we have become so identified with our thoughts, that we can no longer tell the difference between thought and Reality. We also mistake this tool of thought to be what we are. We create a substitute identity made from thought, then we unknowingly hypnotize our mind with that thought created identity and we tell the world, *"I am what I think I am"*. But here's the clinker - we are most definitely not and never will be what we think we are!

Q: How can we attend to Reality whenever we are leading a busy life? I can't find enough quiet time to become present.

A: Look, it does not matter whether you are a busy person, or whether you are a total slacker.

The Real is in all situations and in all places. It all depends upon where your attention is at. Is your attention locked up in La La Land or is it placed firmly in the here and now? The Real is always here and now, it is nowhere else. It is certainly not tomorrow or next week, and it does not rely upon you sitting in some quiet desolate place in order to realize it. The Real is there within your busy work place, and also within your quiet church; it is there when your two year old child is kicking and screaming, and it is there when you are rapt in deep meditation. The Real is everywhere and prevalent throughout the world and the universe at all times. This is still the case, even if your awareness is saturated in thought, instead of paying attention to the real life with Attentive Presence.

It truly is only a matter of where your attention is focused. Is your attention split between the here and now, and what you <u>think</u> of this here and now? Your thoughts and beliefs will always contaminate the here and now, thereby contaminating your true Reality!

Q: But if you live a quiet life, then you haven't got as much going on in your mind. So that should make it easier to become present, shouldn't it?

A: No, not necessarily so. Living an idle life could lead you to spin thought dramas more so, than if you were a busy person. Busy people usually don't have enough time to be spinning lots of silly little dramas in their mind. Someone who lives

an idle life will seek for entertainment to relieve
their boredom. Now what better way to relieve
boredom, than to start dreaming up all manner of
weird thought dramas inside your mind?

What makes awakening easier, is to merely
have the desire for it. You have to be 100%
willing to let go of your thought dramas, that's
all. Once that willingness is in place, then living
with Attentive Presence becomes simple. I used
to think that I had to live a very quiet and boring
life in order to awaken, so for a long time I lived
a very sheltered kind of existence. Of course, this
was when I was hypnotized by false assumptions,
which I received at the hands of some of those well
meaning 'spiritual' teachers we have out there.

We are conditioned to believe that when the
realization of our inner truth dawns upon us,
we will then live sedentary lives with no action
anymore. We also believe that we will hear
trumpets sounding and see fireworks blazing.
This of course is unbridled nonsense. It leads us
to believe that awakening is a super 'achievement'
and requires for us to live a boring life to 'attain'
it.

I found that all I had to 'do' was simply to
listen to life as it was happening all around me.
I listened with _attention_ to all of the sounds I was
making as I worked, or to the sound of traffic as
I walked along a busy street. If I was reading,
I would pay full attention to the words, being
careful not to let my mind drift off into dreamland.
If I was talking to someone, I listened to them

fully, and also to the sound of my own voice as I spoke. I would mainly listen to life, but I would also deliberately feel, see, smell and taste life too. If I was eating, I would deliberately focus on the taste of the food. If I was walking through a forest park, I would take in the smell of the pine trees, or maybe the smell of a barbecue in the distance or whatever else arose. I would feel the wind as it brushed past my face, or notice the warmth of the sun beating down on me.

This diverted my attention away from thought, and took me deeply into the now. So, this is what it really means to live in the now, or to live with Attentive Presence. Then I noticed that thought gradually loosened its grip, and a great sparkle and crystal clear clarity began to emerge in my awareness. As a result, I now see what is, rather than what I think is.

Q: So do you not take any quiet time to meditate or practice relaxation?

A: When people ask me if I meditate, I tell them, "yes I do; 24 hours a day, 7 days a week." *Since meditation is really all about taking your attention beyond thought and uncovering your inner truth, then strictly speaking, you* could *call Attentive Presence a form of meditation. But as for making time for* formal *meditation in the hope of achieving some 'spiritual' goal in the future, well then I would have to say that I don't formally meditate anymore. Though I do have a short power nap most afternoons which I find to* be deeply relaxing, but I don't see any need to get into any funny sitting positions or to formalize it in any way, since I'm just having a bit of a rest really.

There are a few cats which have made my back garden their home, and every time I look out, they are also having a nap. It's funny though; when I watch them having their afternoon nap, I don't get the impression that they are being very formal about it. Cats like to relax in the afternoon, and so do I, mainly because it gives a major energy boost; that's all there really is to it.

Q: But do you not use any mental techniques when you are relaxing like this?

A: I try to live in Attentive Presence at all times, even when I'm having a nap. Now that's the best way to stay relaxed. But when I'm napping, instead of paying attention through the senses, I close my eyes and pay attention within my mind. I simply observe or watch any lingering thoughts which might be floating about; observing them as they come and go. I'm just watching that voice in the head, in an unattached manner. These days it doesn't say very much however. That voice doesn't seem to like being observed, it tends to quieten down all on its own as I bring attention to it. So then the mind naturally clears, and I find that a great depth of relaxation envelopes the body, which is rather nice, since I like the energy boost I gain from this short power nap.

Some people will argue that this is meditation

which I'm 'doing', but to me it is simply a nap. Just because I'm clear and present as I'm taking the nap, doesn't mean I have to stick the label of 'technique' onto it, now does it? All the same, if you do use meditation or a form of relaxation, then by all means continue to use it if you are gaining some benefit from that. We all know that formal meditation has a lot of benefits just as physical exercise has, but awakening is a different kettle of fish altogether.

For example; what happens to your awareness after your thirty minute meditation session is over? Do you drift back into La La Land, or do you stay awake in Reality throughout the day? The truly meditative life is a 24-7 thing, but it's the natural life also. It doesn't take practice, only a _willingness_ to allow your mind to remain clear. Living with Attentive Presence is normal and healthy, whereas having your mind filled up with thought dreams takes work and effort.

Now, when I'm having a nap with Attentive Presence, I get very deeply relaxed, simply because my mind isn't choked with thought. At times when I'm relaxing in the manner I have described, some internal experiences can occur, like hearing inner sounds or voices, or seeing images inside the mind. It gets a bit like watching a movie; you are always wondering what's going to pop up next. So I do recommend paying attention like this, if you are prone to having a nap. Don't just sit back and let your mind wander willy-nilly into La La Land.

This internal observation gives great insight into how thought can hypnotize the awareness; since whilst you are observing thought, you see clearly the dreamlike effect thought has upon your awareness. You then notice how when you are not paying attention, your mind can get saturated in these dreamlike thought scenarios. You will then understand exactly how the mind really works, and how madness can hypnotize the mind quite easily, if you are not paying careful attention to Reality. You'll begin to notice _firsthand_ the difference between thought and Reality. Like I said, it gives great insight into how thought operates. Now, if you want to call that a technique then so be it. I don't call it a technique; I still call it having a nap.

The only thing which causes tension to the body anyway, is getting caught up in the thought content of our mind. So when we use our attention to observe that thought instead, we tend not to get caught up in it so much. The watched pot never boils they say, and it's the same with the mind; the observed mind will never boil with thought. Thought tends to slow down all on its own whenever we are attentive, since thought can only ever saturate our mind when we are _inattentive_ or unawares.

So, when you pay attention like this, you begin to wake up from the thought spell and see Reality as it is, without thought contamination. That's when the Spirit begins to naturally rear its head and come to life within your awareness.

Q: What does it really mean to be spiritually awake?

A: It means that your life experience gets spiritualized. You see what is Real. It means that you regain your natural state of sanity, since being lost in thought is the cause of all the worlds' insanity. It means that you are awakened to the true nature of your Spirit, and also the outer Reality of everything, which is the same Spirit. You realize that all is One. You are the all; you are the One. But awakening is actually very ordinary, even though <u>sometimes</u> it can take your breath away; but it's mostly about keeping your inner space clean of unwanted thoughts and aligning your attention with the Real instead. If there is a breathtaking experience, well that's nice, but an experience is just an experience and it will always go away. An awakened person isn't hooked on momentary experiences, they simply recognize that a thought is just a thought, and so they have a choice of whether to drop the thought, or allow it to spellbind them.

The awakened recognize the un-reality of thought, and as a result of that recognition they don't take it all so seriously anymore. Therefore it's rather difficult to take what people perceive as being an 'ordinary life' seriously anymore.

You'll be, *'in the world but not of the world'*. Have you heard that old statement before – *In the world but not of the world?* It means that you can enjoy the ride, but don't really give a damn about the outcome. To most folk, you'll be seen as being somewhat strange for not giving a hoot about all of the strife everyone else gets so enmeshed in, but what they think won't matter to you any longer. What they think is what they think, right? It's just a temporary phenomenon. Today they think this and tomorrow they think that, right? They are up and down and all over the place with what they think and what they believe, and also the emotions which are a knock on effect of their thinking. It's all just thought stuff they believe in, which isn't at all true. When you awaken, what *you* think won't matter much either, so why the hell would you pay attention to what 'others' think?

It's like when you read a novel, you can get deeply engrossed in the book as you are reading it; you feel the characters emotions and you enjoy the story, but all along you know it is only a story and has absolutely no reality at all – you are un-attached, free and at ease. Awakening is a bit like that; life gets a bit like watching a movie or reading a novel. You will still take pleasure in it, but you find it very hard to take any aspect of it seriously anymore.

It is the ultimate freedom; all of the stress and emotional problems you once had, which came from being so spellbound in your thought story, go straight out the window. Once the un-reality of the thought story is recognized *(truly recognized)*, the burden from that thought story simply drops away from you. It's just like dropping a heavy weight you didn't even know you were carrying. People everywhere are trying to relax nowadays, but if they dropped their thought story and lived life with Attentive Presence, then that relaxation would be automatic. However, that doesn't mean that you will end up being distant from life, or immune to the flow of life's changing current. It just means that things won't get you down, or stress you out too much either. On the other hand, it doesn't mean that you are going to wind up like a stereotypical saint.

Nonetheless, when you see people taking their thought story seriously, it will make you shake your head in disbelief, especially when you see folk spinning thought stories within their mind of what they think is 'spiritual'. We can get so spellbound by spiritual beliefs and different philosophies, it can get quite ridiculous. You may reach a point when you will want to vigorously shake those people, and tell them that the story they saturate their mind with is not real at all. But even when you do tell them that their thought story isn't real, they generally don't listen, because _they want the story_. The thought story amuses and entertains them, and as long as they are obtaining entertainment from their dreaming mind, they will _never_ want to relinquish those dreams and awaken to what is _Real_ – that's just the way it is.

Q: How did awakening change you, or make you different?

A: Awakening is only about waking up and seeing

the truth; it's not about changing yourself or trying to become different. I am one who simply prefers to align my attention with life as it is presented to me, moment by moment. I no longer want to be trapped in thought dreams, since I found all of that to be very tiring, upsetting and quite a bore. I can't be bothered with spinning lots of little thought stories inside my head anymore. Once upon a time, that kind of thing entertained me, but then it all got out of hand and I finally decided to let it go.

So, the weight I had sitting upon my shoulders fell away as I began to live in Attentive Presence. I then began to feel real light, weightless, almost bouncy, and my world brightened up – like someone had turned up the dimmer switch. A very sharp clarity arose in my perception and I then began to feel the oneness of life. There's also a mild electrical energy which vibrates through the body; it's sometimes strong and sometimes weak. When I look at the world around me, it feels like everything is alive and has its own character, even trees, grass and water. I sense that I am looking at myself as I look around me; there's a blending with everything a lot of the time – it fluctuates though.

Thoughts still come and go, just not as much as they used to, and anyway, I now let them come and go, whereas beforehand I kept those thoughts in my mind. As I hung onto those thoughts, I would then expand on them until they grew like a great big snowball inside my head. The pressure of it almost shattered me. So I now prefer Reality over thought, ease over strife and going with the flow of life over constant effort. It doesn't mean that the awakened are special at all; in fact, you could awaken right now if you honestly desired it as much as I did.

Q: What about wisdom - did awakening make you wiser?

A: Anyone who has the ability to learn from their life experience, their mistakes and the mistakes of others, is one who holds the keys to wisdom. The wisdom gained through awakening is the ability to see through the thought show. Then you will know the difference between truth and illusion. You see, wisdom comes from experience, unlike knowledge which mainly comes from books and teachers. We have been conditioned to believe that the awakened are all knowing and all wise – that's a lot of rubbish though. The awakened still make mistakes; however, they are able to learn lessons from making those mistakes.

I don't see myself as being a 'wise' guy. Some so called 'un-awakened' people are far better at playing the whole 'life on earth' gig better than I am, so that makes them wiser in my eyes. I can't do anything apart from go with the flow of life, and run with whatever life presents to me moment to moment, but when I need advice in a particular field I ask for it from those who can give it, even if they are sound asleep in their dreams. So, nobody is all 'knowing' and all 'wise' - and guess what -

neither is your favourite guru, no matter what he says, and if they claim that they are, then they are not awake at all, but completely deluded.

Q: So, even after awakening, we still need advice?

A: Yes we do. Once awakened from the thought spell, you will know that we are all dream characters playing a little game here, but you won't know everything there is to know about that game. I'm sure you'll still want to play a good game, so you'll need to take good advice from those who are well versed in what you require. To me, these people are like God showing me what's next. I just follow the clues and the answers which God gives me. However, those clues and answers do come in very mysterious ways sometimes - I sound very religious now, don't I?

The answers I need usually come through a deep hunch I feel arising within me, but sometimes my directions can come through a book, the television, another person, or even sometimes a child has given me the next clue I need. I listen, I pay attention to life, and I follow the clues, then I take *action*. The action part is always natural and effortless though, even if it requires that I work at something for days, weeks or months, I always have fun operating this way.

That's basically how you live your life in the flow – you wait for God to direct you. You stay alert, so you will recognize the guidance as it comes (by whatever means) and then you move into effortless action.

Q: Do you still live a normal everyday life?

A: Of course I do, I'm not weird you know. I still do all of those things which you and others like to do. I work, I go for walks, I go to the gym, I play golf, I watch movies and I read novels too. Also, if a hammer hits my finger - guess what *- I might let out a hollering yelp, mixed with an obscenity or two!*

Nobody would know that I was even interested in awakening until I started talking about it. By the way – I don't usually talk much about it at all, unless I'm asked about it, mainly because people get all kinds of funny ideas into their heads about how you should be acting after awakening. Many hold childish pictures in their mind of stereotype saints, and then think that's what awakening looks like. I couldn't be bothered explaining my position to people anymore, that's why I wrote it all down in a book. Life goes on and I choose to live it in freedom, so I don't bow to the funny ideas others have concerning how the awakened should act.

Q: What's it like to be awake?

A: Knowing your spiritual truth liberates you from much fear and anxiety, simply because most fear and anxiety is nothing but thought, and you will then have moved beyond thought. Seeing your essence in everything frees you in a way that you can't understand, until you surrender to the flow of life yourself. The word 'awakened' is only a useful word to distinguish between the two different states of consciousness – awake and asleep. If you want to really know what it's like, then you should allow yourself to awaken; that's the only way you'll ever get to know what your true being is really like.

Do you want to know what awakening is really like? Well it's like being *free*, that's really the best word I have to describe it. Now, can your mind imagine that - complete and utter freedom? It's freedom from all of the boring, joyless and stuffy spiritual-religious rules. It's freedom from stress, depression, anxiety and the effort of unending becoming. It is freedom to embrace your natural character and play the game of life like it should be played, with passionate fun!

But it's also most importantly, about coming to know your true nature, as that one indivisible unity which gives birth to all physical phenomena. Realizing that union feels very much like you are dissolving, but it fluctuates, just like egoic consciousness fluctuates, it's not fixed or static at all. Words however will *never* touch this. You have to allow the great clarity of awakening to emerge within yourself, to understand it properly.

Q: What do you mean when you talk about the natural genetic character?

A: I know it's an old cliché, but awakening is a bit like being an actor upon a stage. You know you are only playing a role, and so you willingly play that role, simply because, well, why wouldn't you play it? When you live in the flow, and you are no longer fooled by the role you are playing, then the natural genetic character comes into action without hindrance. It was unhindered when we were children, but then we interfered by making the ego (thought based identity).

Some scientists theorize and have more or less proven that through our genetics we inherit a base personality, or a particular flavour of character. The natural genetic character is derived from a series of genetic programmes you inherited through birth. All of those <u>natural</u> interests, attractions and passions; they appear to be built upon genetic inheritance, which we then build upon when we allow our Spirit to surface and run the show. Spirit uses the natural genetic programming or wiring to play the game of life with. We only ever feel like we are going against the grain or embarking upon an uphill struggle, whenever we are pursuing something which is not in line with our inbuilt genetic character.

But the genetic character is still only a role we are playing. It's natural because it's what our body is wired with, so to speak. It's the experience we as Spirit are seeking to have. But this genetic character isn't totally *real.* What we truly are is something else entirely. Our true inner self is not wholly subject to this genetic wiring, but neither does it oppose it. Instead Spirit will embrace the life giving attributes of the genetic character. Now, the life giving attributes of the genetic character, are those traits which bring true creative delight into our lives. People like Einstein, Tesla or Freud were very much flowing in line with their true character; that's why they were geniuses.

Q: So what's the difference between ego and the genetic character then?

A: When I use the word ego, then I am referring to a thought based sense of 'me' which is not the natural character. The ego is something which we are trying to 'become' because we cannot accept our natural self just as we are. The ego to my mind is hypnosis of sorts. It's what we believe that we are, based upon the worlds influence and conditioning.

Usually when people take to spirituality, they think that they are less attached to the ego than the average Joe Soap. However, because spiritual seekers usually try to conform to a spiritual stereotype behaviour pattern, they actually interfere *more so* with their natural self than the average Joe Soap does. They try to 'become' better people through abiding by religious or spiritual rules of 'becoming'. This is tantamount to becoming something which you are not, usually a saintly type of figure. It is thought based; it's not the natural genetic character.

Really we are Spirit and nothing else is *real*, not even the genetic character. When we awaken, we see through all phenomena, not only the ego but the genetic character as well. We then know that we are pure life. But we need something to play the game of life on planet earth, don't we?

You see the natural character will always be in line with what brings happiness and passion; whereas the ego will find itself doing things mainly for money, prestige, to outdo others or to be seen as being the kingpin. The ego goes against the grain and causes life to be stressful. It has you doing things in life which you hate, like working in a job which you dread. It opposes the flowing river of life. The ego is what I _think_ I am, and what I _think_ I should be, so that the world will accept me as one of its own. It subjugates itself to conformity, like those rats in the old fairytale, which hypnotically follow the tune of the pied piper. So ego is thought based, and it is always trying to alter the natural genetic character, so it can 'fit in' with societies clone like conditioning.

Now, one in touch with the natural genetic character will only dance to their own tune. However, that doesn't mean they will be a rebel, but only that they will be _free!_ With the natural character, you will feel a strong _urge_ to do certain things in life. You could work at those natural urges all day and all night and never get tired. The natural genetic character might follow a life as an artist, a teacher or a musician, but it could also follow a life as a business man or a world leader. It does what it finds fun in, and you may not make much money from what your natural character wants to do, but it will greatly enhance your passion for life. That's what this physical life is all about anyway, learning to live with happiness and passion in _whatever_ you do!

Q: After awakening, could the natural character still do wrong or bad?

A: The natural born character could follow a life of anything at all, but generally, once awakened, you won't find yourself doing things that are detrimental to the world, simply because you'll be beyond thought dramas, which are the only thing which can ever cause detriment to the world. That's the beauty of awakening. You don't have to try to be 'good', you will end up naturally aligned with what we call 'good' – though it won't be the stereotypical 'good' which the religions try to imitate. You'll play your natural role, and then you are no longer a hindrance to others or the world anymore.

At first, you may find that societies clone like mindset might oppose you going your own way and being natural. Some may even hate you, for no longer toeing the line of society's brain washing. Many famous scientists and philosophers etc were fiercely attacked and slandered, simply because they stepped away from the egos world and found their own truth naturally within. Even Jesus met this resistance - mainly from the religious people of his time of course.

But even when playing your natural genetic role; all the while you are totally aware that a role is all it is. Once awakened you won't become lost in it, or identify with the role you are playing in any way. You then look upon the other actors on the stage, and to your awakened mind they look like they are totally hypnotized with the role they are playing. They identify with the character and get lost in the characters story, believing that the play they are involved in is real, and so they cannot distinguish between what is real and what is un-real. On the other hand, one who is awakened can easily distinguish between what is real and what is un-real.

Q: There seems to be a big difference between the awakened natural self, and the un-awakened ego.

A: Yes, there is. An un-awakened person is one who mechanically reacts to every thought which passes through their mind. They are puppets being manipulated at all times by the strings of thought. They are unable to tell the difference between thought and Reality. To the un-awakened, thought is their reality and they usually never question this so called 'reality' at all. To the un-awakened mind, those who do question the un-reality of the worlds thought story are seen as being somewhat mad or weird. Now what a strange situation we are in, whenever insane minds view sanity as madness, yet this is what we are faced with - the insane view the sane as being mad. Now who could possibly find agreement in such a world?

Going with the flow of whatever appeals to you *naturally*, is seen as being a haphazard way of living life, to one who is stuck in their ego. It is seen as being madness, because to the ego you have to plan every little thing in life. The ego wants a five year plan, monthly goals and all of that. The ego doesn't do things because they feel good; it usually has fear of the future, feelings of lack, money or outdoing others on its mind. Yet going with the flow of your natural character will always feel right, good and easy. You'll also enjoy what you are doing, unlike when you do egoic things, which usually winds up making you feel stressed and despondent; like life is a big uphill struggle.

Q: So, we should just accept our natural self, whatever way we find it to be?

A: Yes, but be sure to accept your natural clear mind firstly. Keep your mind devoid of thought dramas, and be attentive to the moment or you will drift into the un-natural state of being spellbound by your thought story. The thought story is not natural, only pure awareness is natural, and then from that pure awareness your natural character is free to come alive. Then you will be free from stress, anxiety or the many mental afflictions associated with being stuck in La La Land.

It is important to accept your natural self, warts and all. Only then will true ease and freedom from tension begin to dissolve. Many spiritual seekers don't want to accept the *'warts and all'* aspects of themselves. They have been conditioned to believe that these aspects of themselves are negative or unspiritual, but whose view of what is negative is right? A religious person might call you negative if you refuse to believe what they believe, or if you break one of their holy laws, or maybe if you laugh or talk to your friend during a prayer service. A stereotype 'spiritual' new ager might call you negative if you eat meat, if you use slang or curse words, or simply if you enjoy an occasional few beers. I've been frowned upon many times, simply because I have said that I have no interest in organized religion. I get shunned because I have called into question the dubious teachings of some gurus. I've also been called negative just for being my natural self. You see, I no longer bow to the rules of religion or to the spiritual dictates of others, and people usually don't like that. People think they need all of these rules and beliefs or the world will go to hell in a hand-basket. But apparently the world is *already* up the creek without a paddle, so we are clearly doing something wrong or the world wouldn't be this way.

The way I see it is quite simple really. If we keep our own mind clear of upsetting thought dramas, then we would no longer be harming anyone else, because we would no longer be mentally harming ourselves. We would naturally be at peace within ourselves. That peace would then be extended out and into the world. This is the only way that the world will truly be at peace. The inner peace has to be allowed firstly, otherwise whatever so called 'peace' the world experiences will end up being very short lived. Now, this peace does not require any beliefs, philosophies or a religious/spiritual list of do's and don'ts. It only requires that we allow our minds to remain clear and free in the ever present now!

But, I guess it all matters what you yourself feel about this. Do you *really* want to be free, or do you want to be a slave to someone else's opinion of how you should be?

Q: Well, I suppose we would all like to be free.

A: Well that's great; then accept yourself as you are, without all of that head stuff which turns your life into a stressful episode of becoming. Only the head stuff, like the beliefs, the philosophies, the spiritual rules and the interfering thought dramas need to be let go of. But it's all just thought at the end of the day; all of this religious/spiritual mind stuff is only thought dramas trying to keep your mind spinning out of control. These thought dramas try to lock you into a prison, where the prison bars are made of beliefs, philosophies, spiritual rules and the effort of unending becoming.

You only have to stop letting that voice in your head ruin your life. Don't listen to it when it says that you are not good enough, or that you have to become this or that. Give that voice the boot. Accept yourself fully, and to hell with what the world and others think of you. Live your life the way you want to, do the unique things that you want to do, pursue your own interests and passions and play your game of life just the way that you were uniquely wired to play it. Accept yourself as you are, and live each day with Attentive Presence – now that's the real key to your spiritual and mental freedom!

7

The Effort Of Becoming

Thought identity:

To be our deepest truth - now what is difficult about that? Surely there is no effort required in being true? Obviously effort is required only in being false. Effort is needed to maintain an illusion of what we like to think we are. Effort is required when we are pretending, or when we are acting the part of something we are not. Effort is needed to uphold the false face of ego, which we try to project upon the world.

When we live our lives from ego, we may feel that it is important for the world to view us in a particular manner. We all want to be liked, loved and accepted by our friends, family and society. So we might feel it necessary to alter our personality, to fit in with the world around us. We might carry around two faces, or maybe three or four faces, depending on whomever it is we are speaking with. This is tantamount to an act we put on for the world; it's like we are actors and the world is our stage. Most of us are putting on the very same act. It's almost as if we are seeking for applause from the world around us, or for the world to tell us, *"Heh, now that you have conformed, we accept you"*.

Maybe applause *is* what we are seeking, so we can counteract our inferior thoughts, and the knock-on feelings of unworthiness we use to dress ourselves up in daily. Could these thoughts and feelings of unworthiness, be the reason why we are always caught up in the effort of trying to become this or that? Could they be the reason why we are always trying to 'become' anything or *anyone* at all, just as long as it is not what we actually are? Are these thoughts and feelings of unworthiness, the reason why we feel compelled to conform, or to fall into line with societies clone like brainwashing?

Why are we always trying to run away from ourselves, by tampering with our natural born character? Why do we throw away that naturally occurring uniqueness of character, which the Spirit appears willing to uphold? We look in so called 'celebrity' magazines and turn to the media, to tell us what is supposed to be 'in' and what's 'out'. Will there ever come a time when we will paddle our own canoes, and find our own way in life, rather than to lean on what the dictates of society have to say all the time? Will there ever come a time, when we will all learn to *accept ourselves* for what we truly are?

Many go to great lengths to build up a false

thought made identity to please or to fit in with what they perceive as being 'others'. But these supposed 'others' are most likely clones of society, more or less. They are also actors, treating you like you are *their* audience. Really and truly, in Reality, they actually are the same source-energy that you are. They are one with you. Strictly speaking, they are you, and you are they!

So stop reading now, and give someone a pat on the back for being a great actor. Tell them that they are maintaining a great act; a grand illusion. It's so grand in fact, that the people of the world are totally spellbound by it all. They don't even realize that they are acting. They think that they *are* what their mind tells them they are. Unbeknownst to them, they really are Spirit in union with God. Many will even fool themselves into believing that the role they are playing is *real*. It can almost get to a point where we play our role so well, that we no longer know with any certainty what our true natural character is like. This is when the mind gets disorientated, and begins to confuse Reality with La La Land.

However, as we try to create a mask of thought identity (ego), which has embedded in it all of the qualities which we think society will accept, what we are actually doing, is creating lots of mental effort, which interferes with our naturally occurring character. We are filling ourselves with fear unbeknownst to ourselves, with the mantra, *"what if they don't like me?"* However, tampering with that pure spiritual nature and natural character gives rise to an illusion, and that is what we meet when we speak to most people in any given day - an illusion!

All folk like to think of themselves in a particular way. We think of ourselves as being a certain type of person, with certain fears, neurosis, complexes and inadequacies etc. We will even go to great effort, exhausting our life energy into 'keeping up appearances' for the friends who we treat like an audience. But all of that thought stuff is not what we truly are. We are that Reality which lies beyond, and gives power to, all of the thought stuff in our mind. And that's exactly what thought identity (ego) is - nothing more than mere thought stuff.

Ego & the natural character:

Ego is the produce of thought conditioning, which we get bombarded with from the world around us. Ego is produced as we mimic our ways of being from the various stimulations we are exposed to, and also from those whom we are surrounded by. Everyone knows how children often imitate people they are surrounded by on a daily basis. This imitation becomes a habit, and soon we find that we have adopted the tastes, beliefs, ways and mannerisms of others, and we then make those tastes, beliefs, ways and mannerisms part and parcel of our thought made identity (ego).

This ego then overwrites our naturally occurring character, and also all of the inborn traits which gives us a sense of uniqueness. We might then grow up feeling like we are being suffocated by the world around us, as we try to conform to what we _think_ we should be. We usually end up doing those things which society tells us we should be doing, and as a result, we find that we are not living in accordance with our own true nature; neither genetic nor spiritual.

This gives rise to stress, depression or a sense of being unfulfilled, simply because we are not living our life in the way we were naturally wired to live it. The ego is an imposter, which is trying to take the place of our natural character; it is trying to drown out the voice of our Spirit and the guidance we would naturally receive from that Spirit. The inner spiritual guidance enlivens us to action, whenever we go with the flow of life, living our lives for the moment. However, the ego is like a form of hypnosis and we are instead hypnotized with thoughts and beliefs, which we now call 'me'. Therefore this has made what we now call our 'personality', very much like a second hand identity.

Yet all the while, the Spirit is trying to live in accordance with the natural body/mind characteristics we were born into this world with. But we keep stifling, pushing down and ignoring the call of the Spirit and of our natural character. We instead listen to what the world has to say about who we should be, or what we should 'become'. So we try to alter our natural self by trying to 'become' what everyone else thinks we should 'become'. We ignore our natural characters talents and passions, and instead we dance to the repetitive and boring beat of society and its clone like monotony of endless becoming.

Now, is that what we really are? Are we this ego which is no more than a mixture of other people and our cultures learning's, living through us in a deeply mechanical and hypnotic manner? Of course, ego shifts and changes to various degrees from year to year. So can something which shifts and changes so much, really be said to be something that is of a true and lasting quality? It's like the weather; one day it's cold and rainy, and the next day it's hot and sunny. So if the weather could talk and claim to have a sense of 'me', what could it possibly say about itself? The impermanence of the rain and sun coming and going, cannot be said to be the true identity of the weather. So it could not say, "*I am hot, cold, rainy or sunny*". The only response or description it could possibly give of itself, from the perspective of its true and lasting quality, would be to simply say, "*I Am!*"

To say "I Am" is the only thing which cannot be disputed. Everything else will come and go, but that sense of 'I Am' never wavers. It is always there, and it is the only thing which will *ever* be true or real. Ego is an attempt to add onto the sense of 'I Am'. Ego says "I am this" or "I am that", which is a false perception of the self. However, to find what is truly real within us, we have to bypass ego, and with our awareness clear, we need to embrace the natural body/mind characteristics. This leaves us awakened to our true natural state, and then life no longer feels like such an up-hill struggle.

The foundations of religion:

Even the world's religions have become infiltrated by the egos need to conform and 'become'. Systems which are meant to bring about spiritual *freedom* and truth to the world, usually only end up as impediments to the awakening which they are meant to facilitate.

Religions for millennia have tried to answer the question of what is real within us. Indeed, some of the original teachers whom these religions were built upon, do indeed appear to have hit upon the answer to that question. Sadly however, when the original teachers died, those who came after polluted and distorted beyond all recognition, the pure teachings which were given by those original teachers. So now, religion no longer appears to hold a *pure* answer to that question of what is real within us. The original teachings will always become twisted, interpreted, re-interpreted and altered to suit the agenda of those followers who wish to organize the original teachings into a new system of conformity. This is how the foundations of organized religion are laid down.

Once the pure teachings of truth become organized, corruption will certainly enter into the mix sooner or later. A grappling amongst the followers for power and control will be the first signs of this corruption. This is when we will see a system of hierarchy being developed within a particular spiritual group, as some of the followers of a particular teacher or guru, seek to become the limelight amongst the other seekers. Those who fail to become the new leaders, usually form a splinter group of some sort, due to this egoic need to be in the limelight. I've seen this time and time again within spiritual groups. Even amongst new age gatherings, the egos need to be seen as being the 'special' one, sooner or later becomes very prevalent amongst _some_ of the original gurus followers. This usually kills the original teachings, which most likely did address that question of what is _real_ within us.

Nevertheless, we can find the answer to the question of what is _real_ within us for ourselves, and indeed that is truly the _only way_ we can ever really find that answer. Since if we are on a search for what is real, then if it's real, it's got to be within us here and now. The only place where the _real_ can reside is within us and all around us – in the here and now!

Some of the modern teachers and gurus of spirituality, although on the surface appear to be interested in focusing upon what is truly real within us, do not appear to hold a _pure_ answer to that question of what is real within us either. Some teachers' words mainly appear to be tainted by what they think everyone wants to hear. Even some of these modern teachers we approach, are putting on that very same act of becoming, which religion and the rest of the world is trapped by in one way or another. It's the 'holy' or 'spiritual' _act_ we see with _some_ of these teachers, but we usually don't want to consider that, now do we?

However, we are the ones who expect them to put on this act, or we will not be impressed with them. We usually don't listen to these teachers, unless they are falling into the stereotypical behaviour pattern we hold within _our mind_ concerning how the awakened should act. So, some of these teachers may feel compelled to play the stereotypical role of the all knowing and 'wise' rishi, simply because _we demand it_ of them.

So now, in order to 'become' what others _think,_ even some teachers will perform for their listeners. If folk are into angels this year, well these teachers will be talking about angels. If the world appears to be interested in crystal healing or afterlife scenarios; well you got these 'teachers' discoursing on crystal healing and the afterlife. Yes indeed; chakras, Chi, spirit guides or levitation; whatever you are interested in this year, you'll have teachers appearing on the scene to supply the goods we demand.

Unfortunately this all falls under the banner of 'spirituality', so one who is seeking for _true_ spiritual awakening, could find themselves distracted by all of these spiritual sideshow issues, instead of focusing exclusively upon _true_ spiritual awakening. This usually leads one down the road of endless 'spiritual' becoming, and if we aren't careful, this road can go on forever, without us ever finding that which we were originally seeking for. This is the road organized religion leads us down.

But we can't blame the priests of religion, or the new age teachers for this, since the majority of humanity still do not want the truth to be delivered to them plainly and unadorned. Let's face it now; the unadorned truth has never gone done well in this world. There have been truth speakers tortured in all manner of ways throughout time. Most of these tortures were carried out by religious institutions. And all of this was for the sole purpose of maintaining the status quo, of spiritual and mental ignorance. But has the world really changed since long ago? Only recently, one of my former teachers was told that he would be killed if he ever returned to Ireland to give a public talk. So now, what do you *really* think - has the world changed?

No - not a bit, is the answer to that question!

The alternative to waking up:

As far as 'spirituality' is concerned, the world appears to mainly want a spiritual sideshow to pass the time away, and _true_ awakening seems to be the last thing that it wants. The world appears to still want the old ways, and it seems that many still want to hide behind belief systems, which at times are tantamount to children's fairytales. Even with the modern new age movement; all that is happening there, is that some people have swapped their birth religion for a 'newer' collection of beliefs. Both religionists and new agers usually hand their power over to outside authorities, rather than to take responsibility for their own mind. The religionists are waiting for God do it all for *'me'*, and the new agers want a guru to do it all for *'me'*.

Both types fall under the sway of philosophy and belief, rather than to let those thought made models of 'reality' go, in order to discover the truth of actual Reality within their own awareness instead. Philosophy and belief are the alternatives which many spiritual seekers and new agers settle for, instead of waking up out of the thought world. And the new agers think that they're being very new and 'radical' by doing this.

Now, anyone who awakens to the Reality of their true spiritual nature will never fall into line with institutionalized and archaic belief systems. They see this as the egos alternative to spiritual realization. The ego does not want to awaken, and it will step in with any old thing at all to keep the dream alive. Religion, philosophy, beliefs and the new age movement provide many alternatives to truth _realization_. The ego will gladly support any old organized system of thought, because these systems will always contaminate and pollute beyond all recognition the pure teachings of awakening. The awakened usually have no time for organized religion, or any kind of belief system at all, because if they did support this kind of thing, then they would be upholding a pseudo 'reality', or a 'spiritual' version of the egos thought world.

Now, the awakened are only interested in stepping outside of the thought world, and *all* of its thought made models, which aim at stuffing Spirit and God into the tiny boxes of our thought made systems of belief and philosophy. The awakened recognize that both belief and philosophy tend to distort the simplicity of awakening, leading those who seek for awakening, to talk and think more about it all, rather than to actually awaken, in the here and now. It leads them to fight against their natural self, as they try to become, or to conform to the dictates laid down by these various systems of *thought*.

It is reported that *even* Jesus went out of his way to deliberately break the religious laws of his time, and he did this right under the noses of the local 'priests'. It appears that he got into a lot of trouble for this of course, just as the *true* teachers of awakening *still* get ridiculed today. It seems that Jesus wanted to highlight the utter folly of the people's belief system, so that they could move beyond it all, and emerge spiritually free in Reality. Obviously it didn't go down very well, just as it still doesn't go down well today (even amongst many spiritual seekers).

But don't get me wrong, the awakened are *not* *against* organized religion either, simply because organized religion and beliefs all fall under the same banner as thought dramas and everything within the egos world. It can certainly help folk for a teacher to point out the delusional manner in which beliefs and thought dramas operate (which is why I'm doing this), but if the awakened took a major stance against all of what arises from the human mind and the egos world, then they would be testifying that the unreal had some kind of Reality to it. If the awakened started taking a stance against all of what is illusory in the world, then it wouldn't be long before they would be back under the sway of the egoic mentality.

This could happen very easily, since when you see the truth, you also get to see the lies which you were once so spellbound by, and it's hard to keep quiet about this when you do awaken. You really feel like shaking people awake, or hitting them with a stick like the old Zen masters would do. However, awakening brings in its wake the ability to _see through_ all forms of delusion, so generally there is no real desire to start taking a stance against this stuff, because it would be like fighting with a mirage. And anyway, the majority wouldn't listen to you, simply because the 'believers' don't like having their _comforting_, 'safe' and 'secure' picture of 'reality' tampered with.

However, I always maintain that nobody is a Superman, even those who have allowed awakening to occur within themselves. At times you can get so bombarded with the mindless trivia you hear emanating from within this world, that if you were exposed too much to it, and you were not totally watchful, you might sometimes feel yourself being pulled a little into the egos world of silly mind stuff once again. Though rest easy, because you won't be pulled in totally, because if your overall preference is for Reality, then the weight of your desire should keep you firmly upon Reality's track. The awakened mainly ignore or overlook the egos world, its thought dramas and its belief systems. They realize that it is all like a mirage, which you can gaze upon and be fooled by if you were _momentarily_ unawares, but there is no way that you will be fully sucked into thinking that it is all real.

Now, I apologise to those religious/spiritual minded folks if this angers you. I remember what it was like when someone called my 'once upon a time' belief system into question, and it hurts. But heh, the truth hurts those who are not ready to hear the truth. It's about time the world realized that _true spiritual awakening_ is about realizing the truth within your own awareness _experientially._ When this occurs, you no longer need belief, simply because you have gone far _beyond belief_ in all respects!

No belief has any truth to it, because belief is mere thought. Spirit holds the only truth there is, and this fact is not a belief but a living Reality!

And so, the world has many religions and philosophies which do not serve the truth at all, but merely serve the interests of the guys who pitch those philosophies to the world. This all keeps the wheel of becoming spinning never-endingly. It keeps us all forever chasing after our true spiritual nature, seeking everywhere, apart from within ourselves, where we can truly find that spiritual Reality. And when we do finally allow ourselves to step outside of the delusions in order to find our Reality, we will see clearly that these systems only attempt to keep us busy with the endless 'becoming' of something that we are not, whilst pushing out of our awareness the _ALL_ that we are!

8
We're Not Worthy

Freedom or slavery:

Iwould like to ask that you pause for a few minutes before you continue reading. For your own benefit, please take a moment to consider an honest answer to the following question.

What do you really want,

spiritual freedom or slavery?

I know, I know; at first glance it appears to be a pretty weird kind of question to be asking. The answer seems obvious, doesn't it? Or is the answer really as obvious as it appears, I wonder? For example, do you see yourself as a slave to thought or as the master of your own mind? It appears rather arrogant to be claiming to be the master of your own mind, doesn't it? Heh, you could even be accused of having a big ego for making a remark such as that.

But the truth is that awakened folk *are* the

masters of their own mind. So if you feel that you are not _worthy_ enough to start being the master of your own mind, then you *really* have no business seeking awakening in the first place. If you feel that being the master of your own mind is an arrogant thing to be claiming, then you are subscribing to a form of spiritual slavery, which will be kept in place as long as your feelings of unworthiness persist. Deception breeds even more deception. When you feel unworthy and _believe_ in that unworthiness, then your feelings of unworthiness will grow stronger; it's a vicious circle. That is, until you break the pattern of course, and then become arrogant enough to say, *"Yes, I am ready to be the master of my own mind!"*

Awakening isn't a game that you can play with, and it isn't something for the bored and the restless to entertain themselves with. Victimhood and beliefs in unworthiness have no place within an awakened mind. Your victim mentality has to be put out with the trash if you really want to wake up _now!_ So, getting back to the question I asked - well, do you want spiritual freedom or slavery? Have you honestly considered what your answer is? Have you even considered the implications of your answer?

Your answer, providing it is a true answer and not one thrown out by the ego, is going to provide real clarity to establish if you are actually _ready_ for spiritual awakening or not. The only prelude which is necessary for awakening to occur is whether or not your readiness is in place. Your readiness is simply based upon the strength of your *desire* for awakening, and that alone. It has nothing whatsoever to do with how many gurus you have visited or how many 'spiritual' books you have read. It has no relationship with how many koans you can unravel, or how well you can recite sutras or various spiritual discourses. You could have been a spiritual seeker for many, many years, and may still not be willing to move beyond philosophy and the daydreaming mind in order to enter your Reality.

On the other hand, you could be an alcoholic or a drug addict and this could be the very first book you have ever read on the subject of spiritual awakening, and your readiness and willingness could be 100% perfectly in place.

We tend to think that just because one has been meditating every day for twenty years, then that makes them a perfect candidate for awakening. But this is not the case at all. The best candidate for awakening is one who has reached the end of their tether with the internal fantasy land of thought. It is when you grow somewhat weary of the content within your mind that you tend to look elsewhere for a better way. Have you ever had a bad day and found yourself thinking, *"There's got to be a better way."*

Readiness is based upon how much you *want* that better way. It is also based upon how much you desire peace. You might not have ever meditated in your life, but if your readiness to make that small shift of attention from thought to life is *absolute*, well then, you might awaken whilst an ardent meditator may not. So an honest answer to that question, of whether you want spiritual freedom or slavery, is going to set the foundation for whether or not awakening is ever going to happen for you. Until you make a firm internal shift or decision, between Reality and fantasy or freedom and slavery, then all you can really hope for is a few momentary spiritual experiences every once in a while.

Abiding realization comes from that powerful decision to opt for Reality over your daydreaming mind. That decision helps us to see through the charade that is the thought world. When we see through the charade, we tend not to take it seriously anymore, and therefore, it no longer has any impact upon our perception. When we make that firm decision, based upon a knowing internal feeling that we have reached the end of the line where the ego is concerned, then and only then, can we see the light at the end of the tunnel we have been living in.

Your answer to the question I have asked is the choice between fantasy and Reality, ego or Spirit and the truth or mere philosophy. It is the decision to awaken to your true nature, or to remain asleep in daydreams. However it must be emphasized that the decision cannot be made with the thinking mind (ego), but it is more a *certainty of feeling* which comes to you, when you know for sure that you are finally ready to move out of La La Land and into the now of life, as it is.

Now, unless we opt for spiritual freedom, then we really are like willing slaves; slaves to the mechanical thought process which we willingly allow to contaminate our pure awareness. Now, I assume that everyone who reads this will most likely jump in with the answer, *"I want spiritual freedom!"* But I wonder, do you really? As a possible spiritual seeker, do you really want to let go of the willing slavery? How much of your daydreaming mind are you ready and willing to let go of? How much do you value the prospects of spiritual freedom?

Well I guess the answer all depends upon whether we like the egos pain, stress and discontentment, or whether we prefer the Spirits peace, happiness and inner fulfilment. Seems like a pretty straightforward choice doesn't it? We might assume that surely everyone wants peace, happiness and inner fulfilment, but take a look at some people and see how they appear to get a kick out of upsetting themselves and everyone else around them. I have observed that some people will always opt for a stressed out frame of mind, full of trash thoughts. I don't know, maybe it makes an otherwise uneventful life appear to be a little less boring.

Some folk also like to indulge in feeling unworthy of the Spirit, as they perpetually play the role of the victim. Even when all is going well in life, these types will search for something to rock the boat. So it may be unwise of us to assume that surely everyone would choose spiritual freedom over slavery. Even a lot of spiritual seekers want to hang onto a victim mentality, rather than take responsibility for their own mind and life. I guess these types find it a lot easier to blame God or others for everything negative that happens in their life, rather than to take a good long look in the mirror, heh?

For some spiritual seekers, reading spiritual books and attending sessions of what has been called 'satsang', is really nothing more than a hobby to them. Many will still prefer to derive their familiar sense of 'me' from the habitual discontentment of their perceived heavy 'past'. The heavy 'past' of course, is just nothing more than thought dramas rattling around within their mind, but try telling some of them that! It's like trying to take an unwilling junkie off their heroin. If the junkie doesn't 100% really _want_ to get off the heroin, in the long run, it isn't going to happen. It's exactly the same for the spiritual seeker. If you don't _totally_ desire the freedom of spiritual awakening over your thought dramas, then in the long run, it also isn't going to happen!

Like the puppet on a string, most of us are at the mercy of, and are subject to, the pull of hypnotic thought dramas which we might _refuse_ to even question the so called 'reality' of. We might refuse to question these inner dramas, simply because we find them to be so damned entertaining; like something major is always going down with 'me' and my 'life'.

Through awakening, it becomes quite evident

that _nothing_ major is ever going down. It's all just thought dramas playing tricks in your awareness!

So the answer to the question, of whether we want spiritual freedom or slavery is an important one. It allows for us to get _real_ with ourselves, possibly for the first time. When we finally get real with ourselves, and establish within our mind whether we actually do want to let go of our victimhood, or whether we want peace rather than stress, Reality over fantasy, or the truth over a mere philosophy – it is only then that the way can finally be cleared for spiritual takeoff (so to speak).

Beyond belief:

Do you feel unworthy of the Spirit? Many folk do, simply because most of us were brought up in a religion, which led us to believe that we were all a bunch of 'sinners'. I recall at the age of seven; I and my fellow class mates at school were told by our teacher that we were all born as 'sinners', so none of us could ever claim to be 'good'. Even at the age of seven, I recognized this as being a whole lot of old rubbish, so I naturally didn't accept it. However, I recall that most of the other boys in the class _did_ accept it at this time.

We were asked by the teacher to stand up in front of the class if we considered ourselves to be 'good'. So at this young age, I was the only one in the class who was 'arrogant' enough to stand up and tell the teacher, _"Heh, I am good"_. But the teacher rather angrily told me that I had better sit back down again very quickly or 'else' – so naturally I sat back down again.

I noticed repeatedly throughout my life that a lot of religious people, and indeed many 'new age' spiritual seekers, tended to get rather angry when you disagreed with their beliefs of unworthiness. Eventually it became shockingly clear to me, that their beliefs were simply a form of hypnosis. Belief is a mixture of thought and concepts which we take on board without any proof. Now, our beliefs could be erroneous, but we don't even _want_ to consider that, now do we?

Well let us see; test yourself here and now. Do you find a little irritation arising within you as I say that your beliefs are a form of hypnosis? Don't you realize that the irritation comes from having a fixed opinion about something, which you have allowed to _saturate_ your mental awareness? You have made that opinion a part of your psychological 'me' (ego), and when that opinion or belief is questioned, you will usually feel like you are being personally attacked. However, if our awareness is saturated in any form of thought, then we cannot really claim to be genuinely _free_. We are a puppet being dangled by the puppet master of thought identity (the ego)!

Now, I'm not asking you to agree with me here, because then you would be caught up in _believing_ again. I am suggesting however, that maybe you try to be brave enough to do a little digging within your own psyche for a change. Perhaps you think that _your_ beliefs are true? Well, where is your proof that they are true? If you had proof then they would no longer be beliefs. If we had proof they would be certainties, wouldn't they?

Now, don't allow yourself to get frustrated by the questioning going on here - this is really a good thing to be doing. This type of questioning brings great clarity, because when we question the thoughts (beliefs) we hold, then we might actually have a chance of seeing beyond those thoughts, and then discovering actual Reality where the _true_ Spirit is to be found. The true experience of Spirit is quite literally, _beyond belief!_

Now, religion for example, does a great deal of promoting the idea of spiritual unworthiness throughout the world. We, as simple folk tend to suck this in, and we become somewhat hypnotized by it. At times it seems to me, that we as a species get a secret thrill out of these feelings of lowliness and unworthiness. It is somewhat disconcerting that in today's world, if we even admit that we _love_ ourselves, it is frowned upon. What then, are we supposed to hate ourselves instead?

However, when we realize that it is only our thoughts which create the facade of unworthiness and limitation we appear to hold so dear, what are we going to do about it? Do we enjoy feeling like a victim? Is there really some kind of secret thrill we get out of feeling limited and unworthy of the Spirit? Are we going to continue weaving this tapestry of discord within our mind, or are we going to simply let it go?

When we do decide that we want peace, happiness and inner fulfilment, we can simply align our attention with Reality. We can then divert our attention away from the heavy and dead useless baggage of thought we may have been carrying around within, and direct that attention through our _senses_ towards life as it is - the here and now!

Upon hearing this, many who claim to want spiritual awakening, will steadfastly claim that it's not just as simple as that. But don't you know deep down that _it is as simple as that_, but we firstly love to play a little game of cat and mouse, don't we? We enjoy the spiritual search; the game of 'catch me if you can'. It keeps the _'we're not worthy'_ mentality ongoing. It keeps the game going. There's nothing wrong with all of that of course, it's still just another dream, but then those who enjoy dreams will never want Reality. They would much rather remain asleep, dozing in a fluffy little dream called 'spiritual seeking'.

Waking up from La La Land is only based upon which seems more agreeable to you; your daydreams or the prospects of awakening to your true spiritual Reality. You only have to be willing to accept that you _are_ good enough for this realization. You most certainly _are_ worthy of the Spirit, since it is what you _actually_ are. It is what's _Real_ within you, and the thought dramas you have been fooling yourself with are most certainly not real!

Once you are finally 'arrogant' enough (like

me) to accept that you are worthy, then accept this also - it is not hard to pay attention to where you are. It is not hard to fully experience life through each of your senses right _now_. Is it really that hard to listen to what is happening, here and now? Is it difficult to see, smell, taste or feel? Surely it can't be difficult to divert your attention into one of these senses, is it? It only takes a little willingness for it to happen. It is not difficult, nor does it take any time at all to switch your attention out of the fantasies, and to divert that attention into the present Reality, to experience simple life, with sensory aliveness, just as it is.

We do not need to grow a beard like the gurus do; we do not have to memorize a whole pile of spiritual philosophy, believe anything, nor wear a white robe, or erect a make shift halo around our head. There is no need to speak in a false calm voice, burn incense, construct a sacred alter, erect a statue to a deity, quote a famous Guru's words or to sit in a certain position, to simply live with Attentive Presence in the now!

Due to a misunderstanding, we may feel that we have to become a so called 'special' person to make ourselves worthy of our true nature. We listen to the gurus words and read spiritual texts, and we may then glean an underlying impression that these teachers are _more_ than what we are. Yet any honest speaker on the subject of awakening, will always speak of awakening as being the true natural state of _everyone_!

To pay attention to each unfolding moment

and to embrace life fully; who said one needs to be a special person to 'do' that? How special does one have to be to simply appreciate the song of a bird? How mystical do we have to become, in order to fully enjoy a pleasant walk through the park upon a summers evening? What beliefs or spiritual training are necessary to breathe deeply, and appreciate the crisp air upon a hazy autumn morning? Where is it written that we require special initiation or higher knowledge to merely be what we are - where we are?

Really, it's all as easy as ABC. I challenge anyone to present to me a clear rationale for the difficulty we are supposed to endure in order to be as we are, and simply switch our attention into life, just as it is. There is no spiritual development necessary to merely experience life fully in each and every moment. There is no longwinded or taxing intellectual understanding required, for each of us to embrace the ordinariness of every now. What effort is there in *letting go* of the defective control stick of thought, which we have been turbulently running our lives with, and to flow with the refined and care free stream of life instead?

Did we not all do that as children? Did we as children not naturally play the game of life the way all games should be played, with fun, light heartedness, ease, in peace and in joy? When did we stop allowing ourselves to savour life? Why do we want our lives to be a continuous struggle, just so we can fool ourselves into believing that we are 'becoming' something in the eyes of the world? When did we all start beating ourselves up, with all this trash about being 'sinners' and about being unworthy of God? Most of us hand over _all_ of our energy to trash thought dramas and delusional beliefs.

"Let's drink to world peace" many people say. Now, how can world peace ever come about whilst the people of the world have their minds in utter turmoil? The ego keeps rehashing the past, and it doesn't care if the past was hellish as long as it is familiar. Familiarity keeps fear at bay, so in an attempt to block out fear, the ego will always keep the past repeating itself. It will just keep repeating the same old monotonous patterns until it grows weary of it all, and is then perhaps _finally_ ready to look for that better way, which is the easiest of all ways.

So, are you finally ready to _really_ look for that better way?

The slavery of La La Land:

Contaminating our everyday conscious awareness is a collection of thought which makes slaves of us all. We willingly march to the repetitive beat of these thoughts; this inner tyrant which has become known throughout the world as the ego. As we march to the egos insidious beat, we suffer the emotions which emanate from the dictates of that inner oppressor. Perhaps those thoughts and emotions will make us feel like we are less than we know we can be. Maybe those dejected feelings will hold in place our belief of unworthiness, and our inner conviction that we are not good enough for the realization of our true spiritual nature.

Recalling from my own life, a time when I was afflicted with this slavery; I can now safely say that I would rather disintegrate into oblivion than to _choose_ going back to filling my mind with this kind of garbage thought. We fill our minds with darkness and then we seriously wonder why we cannot find a light within the world. Is it any wonder we feel unworthy of the Spirit? But we are not unworthy of the Spirit since _we are that Spirit_ anyway. So how can we be unworthy of what we already are?

I guess that most folk don't really want to give up the inner thought demons anyway, since the inner demons of thought can sometimes make life seem a bit like a ride upon a fairground ghost train. Yes to be sure, the ghost train can be scary and stressful but it's also exciting. I theorize that it's only when we spend too much time upon the ghost train, and the demons get a tad overpowering and out of hand, that we might _finally_ bring about a state of zero tolerance. We may then become very much opposed to the pain these inner demons are causing us. I feel it is only at that time, when we will really want to let these thoughts go, and opt for the better way instead.

But we are so used to playing the heavily rehearsed fictional character we have been superimposing over our true nature; we are hypnotized with the thoughts emanating from it. We are also so identified with the human body as being what we are, that our truth appears hidden from us. Yet the truth is not hidden; this is a lie! The truth is always there, within us and all around us, and we only have to shake off the lies, and then pay attention to the truth instead for this realization to hit home.

What we place our attention upon grows within our life, and what we take our attention away from, dies within our life. Now, when I say pay _attention_ to the truth, that's exactly what I mean. I don't mean to read a lot of philosophy, in an attempt at trying to figure out the truth of Reality with our thinking mind. The truth of Reality stands way beyond anything the thinking mind could ever conjure up. The truth of our Reality can only be lived and experienced – _not thought about!_

Philosophy is just like any other hobby in the world, it can be extremely enjoyable tearing Reality apart and stripping it down into segments with endless ideas and concepts. But we have to go beyond thought, in order to discover that which thought cannot touch. Thought is based upon what we know, it is divisive and it names and labels everything, thereby turning a natural unity into a seeming duality. Even to be speaking of the true nature of Reality is to cut it up into pieces, since words have to be used to describe it. Since language is just more thought, well then, we cannot accurately use language to describe that which is beyond what language has the ability to express.

I cannot even accurately express the realization of our truth here within this book, since the realization of truth is experiential in its nature. All we can really do concerning the expression of truth realization is to try using language to the best of our ability, to inspire others who may want the realization of truth to occur within their own awareness. Yet, once the simplicity of awakening to our true nature is recognized, we must lay aside philosophizing and theorizing, because this will only serve to distract us from moving naturally into that present spiritual Reality.

The persistent study of gurus' writings, the constant search for techniques and the relentless reciting of second hand wisdom, all merely serve to make that which is the simplest of all attainments, appear as being the most difficult of all attainments. And when it seems difficult, well then, I suppose the endearing thought of *'We're not worthy'* will persist forever.

Yet, surely any difficulty would be in the effort of upholding a lie, and not in the realization of a truth? The awareness of our truth should only require a falling away of all the lies of thought. With awakening bringing about the _seeing through_ of these inner lies, the end result of that seeing through, is that we choose not to place our attention upon these lies anymore. We then choose to place our attention with sensory aliveness upon _Reality_, and subsequently, a re-emergence of spiritual awareness arises within us.

Take your attention away from that which is false, and direct it toward that which is true, and what do you get? You get the realization of thee absolute truth!

To _think_ that I am, rather than to _be_ what I am; this is the lie which needs to fall away. We maintain this lie throughout each and every day, as we willingly allow our attention to drift off to sleep in La La Land. We dream up fantasy situations and inner worlds within our mind, which correspond to nothing that is real. In the thought world that is La La Land we can repeat over and over, again and again, all of our favourite annoyances, our fears, our grudges, our regrets, our inferiorities, our angers, our philosophies and, _oh yeah_ – let's not forget our good times too!

La La Land is a world we construct within our mind; a world made of thoughts. It is the world we dream up as a replacement for Reality. It is the world as we would either prefer it to be, or the world as we fear it might be. It is the world of our worst fears and secret feelings of inadequacy. We look out through our thoughts and into the world, and all we see is our thoughts projected outward, colouring everything and everyone we meet. Truly, until we allow ourselves to awaken to our spiritual truth, all we will ever see is our own thought projections.

The world masked with thought; it is this which I call La La Land. It is the land of the un-real, the land of the sleepwalker and the land of the ego. It is here in this dream world where we will find all of our fears and depressions, and all that we believe to be 'me' (the ego) - that unreal fictitious phantom of the imagination.

Let this thought world go from our awareness, and then there will finally be some space left for Spirit to emerge – *it's that simple!*

9
Where the flow don't go, I don't go!

Union with life:

Deep down we all want to experience once again the natural unity of life. All of our hankering after happiness and seeking for connection with 'others', is merely a reflection of that innate desire to awaken to our true state of union with Life/God. The need to feel united as one is coming from a deep place within us, which we have possibly never even conceived of, since it's coming from the Spirit within us. And yes, it is a genuine feeling to want to be united, but the ego interprets that feeling in its usual way, which is through thought. So instead of allowing the union of the Spirit to surface within us as it should do, we usually settle for the egos thought made type of unity as a substitute, or a compromise.

What do we do then, instead of wake up to the natural unity of life? We usually get very patriotic about our nationality, or we support a football team, or a particular religion. Then we say, *"Together we stand, united as one"*. But these ego attempts at union will not work because thought cannot join, hence the divisions and bitter rivalry we find amongst nationalities, religions and football teams etc. Only the Spirit is truly in union with all of life, and when we are attentive to that true Spirit within, then we experience that true union, which always was the case, but we were just too distracted by thought to pay any attention to it.

In our inner recesses we all want this spiritual union (even the Hitler's of the world), but most of us would rather settle for the egos substitute for union, simply because we do not remember, or even know of the great peace and deep release there is whenever we return to awareness of the Spirit within us. We do not trust that the Spirit will make our everyday lives lighter, peaceful and more care free. So we cling desperately to the steering wheel of our lives, not giving the Spirit a chance to brighten things up for us. Due to our lack of trust in that Spirit within, we feel that we can plan for our peace and happiness even better than the Spirit can. We think that we can imitate unity or oneness, with our egoic substitutions.

For awakening and true unity to survive within you it requires trust, for you are literally handing over control of your life to your inner higher power. I say 'higher' because this power is of the Spirit, which knows how to live better than your ego does. The ego usually hasn't got a clue whether it is coming or going, hence the reason why ego and that sense of being unfulfilled usually go hand in hand. Through awakening you will be letting go of the defective control stick you have been turbulently running your life with. _You_ are that higher power. That higher power is within you as your true nature, so really you are handing over control of your life to your true self. The ego is not your true self; it is an alteration we make, or a substitution for our true nature. It requires effort and energy to maintain it because it is literally not _true_, therefore it also requires control.

Usually we have a tight grip upon our lives, trying to control every aspect of it. As we attempt to plan for the future we usually get tense, stressed and fearful, due to our being afraid that we will screw it all up. So therefore, with awakening to survive within us, we need to give up this control and _trust_ that our inner truth can do a better job. All of those personality defects which we are constantly fighting against or trying to subdue, no longer exist whenever we live from our true nature. Our Spirit, in Reality, is unstained by the blemishes of the thought entity, and this truth becomes quite obvious as we allow awakening to occur.

But instead of trusting and flowing with the Spirit; as another alternative, many spiritual minded people will instead often hanker after ways to control, or to _make their lives work_. They are always digging into their past and seeking methods to heal that illusive 'inner child'. They struggle to do all kinds of work – body work, energy work, mind training and working out karma etc. Listening to them, would make one feel that life is really supposed to be some kind of a big old boring and joyless chore, instead of the great adventure it was meant to be.

I know this from experience, because this is exactly how I was, whenever I was one of those forlorn spiritual seekers. I had my hands strongly clamped around the steering wheel of life. I felt at that time, that if I let go of all the control I would wind up adrift in the world, lost like a piece of flotsam upon a bumpy wave. Yet the weird thing was, that as a result of this tiring control, I and my outer life always remained a mess - in a fragmented state. I felt isolated from everyone, from the world at large, and certainly from what we call God, or what I now call Reality!

It wasn't until I switched into Reality, and gave up all of the control over everything in my life, that life became progressively more enjoyable and peaceful. I then began to sense the _true unity_ and oneness of all life. Looking at the life forms around me felt strangely like I was looking at myself. I could see the same life essence embedded within everything; even in water, trees, dogs and cats, in the clouds and the very air itself. Life literally came to life, whenever I let go and shifted my attention into the now. I realized that I shared this essence with everything. Indeed in Reality, I _actually_ was this everything. It felt at times like I was dissolving into the air around me, blending with the whole. I could see the sparkle of Life/ Spirit everywhere!

The clarity and crystal clear awareness which arises whenever we allow the mental clutter to subside, is truly wonderful. It is also a relief when we realize that the Spirit can turn our life into a more pleasing journey, whereas the controlling ego tends to suck all of the fun from life, and generally mucks it all up. It truly is a welcomed release to be able to give up the control, and then hand the reigns of life back over into the hands of our Spirit, where they should have been all along!

Nonetheless, seekers seem to have an under riding belief that all is not well, and that they have innumerable inner demons to slay and problems to overcome, before they can let go and join in with the flow of life in this care free manner. However, is it any wonder this kind of belief is held, whenever we listen to some of the teachers out there, who seem hell bent on making us feel like we are not worthy of the Spirit. Even the new age crowd have the _belief_, that we have dark corridors within ourselves, which we need to traverse before awakening can ever happen.

Even after many 'new agers' have turned their backs on organized religion, they might still feel it necessary to carry out some very religious practices; like renouncing the world to become spiritually 'perfect', due to the lingering fear of 'Gods' opinion upon us. Maybe we even feel that being 'perfect' is the only way to enlightenment or spiritual awakening. But let me ask you a simple question – do cats, dogs or birds worry about being perfect? Of course they don't; they are happy to be the carefree expression of life as it is, flowing with the moment, expressing themselves as nature, life and as God intended.

You won't see your pet dog fasting or running around renouncing their bone. I don't think cats are into penance of any sort. I used to have a budgie, and I never once witnessed him begging God to forgive him for being a miserable sinner. However, my budgie did occasionally bang his head on the bars of his cage, and more than once his head would bleed; maybe that was his attempt at flagellation, I can't be totally sure.

Let's take children now for an example. I'm pretty sure that you won't find many children beating themselves up for being 'imperfect'. Children are usually free of all that nonsense until the 'all-knowing' adults of the world inform them differently. Small children are already in union with what we call God, and they are already flowing with life's smooth current. That is of course, until the various education and belief systems of humanity 'educate' them to 'know' better.

Once we move into the egos world, out comes the list of do's and don'ts, out comes the rules and regulations of society and religion; the dictates, the demands and the suffocating pressure to 'become' what everyone else thinks we should become. We then begin to live the life of others, rather than to follow our own natural instincts and intuition, flowing with life in our own unique way. We enter the egos La La Land, and once inside the egos prison house of thought we neglect the Spirit, as we try to 'become' something within the egos world.

We stop flowing with life and grip the steering wheel of life tightly, ever fearful that if we don't control everything, our world will crumble in around us. We forget that God or the Spirit can render our experience in life to be perfect in all respects. But our trust in the Spirit usually gets smothered by the egos world of becoming, and it is that very _trust_ which has to be in place, before we awaken to our true spiritual nature, and to discover the flow of life and union with God once again!

All is well:

Awakening brings the realization that we are perfect just as we are. Anything which we may deem to be 'bad' only emanates from being lost in the thought world. When we emerge from the thought world and come to life in the *Real* world, we understand that all is perfect and all is well. We then stop taking this temporary life so seriously.

Really, that's the main reason for many of the world's problems – being lost in the thought world. Once lost inside the world of thought, we tend to take things far too seriously. We ignore the vibrancy of life which is within us and surrounding us here and now. Whilst we are busy thinking and philosophizing about life, *Real* life waits unbeknownst to us. It waits only for our invitation to allow life to be as it is. It dares us to peek out at the *Real* world, to look out from under our belief systems and philosophies. It merely asks that we leave behind the thought world wherein is contained all of our fears, regrets, depressions, grudges, angers and all manner of neurosis. It asks us to choose simple Reality over La La Land and the egos materialistic lifestyle, and dare to consider that all is indeed well.

It is because we are taking a game far too seriously, that we don't see this. It is because of our seriousness, that we support the world's conflicts and find ourselves as slaves to the egos money rat race. This game called 'life', which can become such a source of stress when directed by the ego, causes us this stress and psychological pain, because we refuse to accept that this game meets with a <u>*dead*</u> end, quite literally! At first glance it sounds like I am being downbeat in saying this, but I'm not really. This awakened realization carries with it great liberation from all that is false, and from all that doesn't really matter at the end of the day. It means that we can play our game of life and enjoy it fully without attachment, demands or dependence upon a particular outcome, just the way we were meant to!

As we recognize that 'life' is only a game, the stress, effort, pain and seriousness goes out of it all. We no longer demand from life, and we no longer wait around refusing to be happy, until we 'become' what the ego has deemed to be a 'success'. The deep understanding that the game of life on Earth meets with a dead end, usually strikes us before we allow a total awakening to the only point of life that matters – that point being _now_!

Maybe you disagree with me, maybe you think that the 'life on earth' gig is a big serious thing, but you know, once awakened you probably won't see it that way, because it's a bit hard to take the whole 'life on earth' thing seriously, whenever you can see through it all as easily as you can see through a dirt-free windowpane. The ego tries to attract our attention with its little trinkets and trappings, and this is how it measures 'success' in life. Of course, the egos version of 'success' (the rat race) usually goes hand in hand with fear, anxiety, stress and feelings of worthlessness. At its worst, our life could become a living hell whenever we dance to the tune of the ego, and choose its world view over the Spirits.

Really, at the end of the day - We shouldn't take life so seriously, because life doesn't take _us_ all that seriously!

After awakening, the whole 'life on earth' thing is viewed as a passing show. You may be shocked as you will then see clearly how people are so spellbound by thought made characters, playing their heavily ingrained roles, thinking that the body is what they are. Everyone is caught up in playing a game, which they don't recognize as being just a game. When you wake up from your trance of thought, you will still respond to the game, but then again, you will still respond to losing money in a game of monopoly, but you aren't really fooled into thinking that the game is real, are you? Awakening out of La La Land leaves one viewing the so called problematic 'big serious life' in that manner. Problems then get a bit like losing money in a game of monopoly. This is where going with the flow of life enters. When all of the struggle to become this or that ceases and we give up, surrendering to life's flow, releasing our hand from the control stick, and then placing our trust in the Spirit to guide us, we usually find an ease and lightness in everything that we do. We also find that illusive _better way_ of living, which the majority of humanity craves to find.

Nonetheless, most spiritual seekers still seem to mistrust and be unwilling to surrender to the Spirit within (which is that better way). They appear to be forever with their hands gripped tightly upon the steering wheel of life. They might say that they have surrendered to a higher power, but they sure as hell haven't really surrendered. They are very much in control, since they are always trying to 'become' clichéd spiritual people, instead of releasing this need to 'become' and instead allow themselves to realize the true Spirit which they are.

I dare you to let this effort of becoming go, and step out of the egos world. I dare you to accept that you _are_ good enough for union with God. I dare you to accept fully your true spiritual nature, and I dare you to realize that all is indeed well.

Our natural wiring:

Seekers are ceaselessly building up a so called 'process' of some sort; a process of endless spiritual 'becoming'. They are always trying to realize the truth of their true nature, by trying to become someone else or something other than their true nature. They are always trying to get to the now by avoiding the now - *"I will be in the now, sometime tomorrow"*; that is the underlying mantra of many spiritual aspirants. Anything will do as long as it does not involve being your true self, as you are, here and now. They will latch onto a philosophy, a belief system, a spiritual group, a holy book, a religion or a guru – anything at all, to avoid the sheer simplicity of aligning ones attention with the present moment where Reality is to be found.

So now, I guess certain questions have to be answered - are you done putting off the now until that illusive tomorrow? What about all of that philosophy; are you ready to peek out from under it all, to see if you can discover the truth yourself, in your own experience? Are you really ready for letting go of the mental noise, in order to awaken to the Reality of your true situation? If you are, then I speculate that I'm writing for the right type of person here.

However, most seekers who claim to be interested in awakening to Reality, aren't really interested in pure awakening. They are really only interested in finding more and more methods of 'making their lives work'. Of course there is nothing wrong with that, but you have to realize that being awakened means that you tend to go with the flow of life. As Jesus is recorded as stating; once awakened you tend to, *"take no thought for tomorrow, for tomorrow takes thought for the things of itself"*.

Now, trying to 'make your life work' is not going with the flow. Trying to 'make your life work' involves exerting great effort and control over everything in life. But you cannot be in control of everything in life, and also leave it up to the flow-Spirit at the same time. Your hands are either on the steering wheel or off it. Awakening involves taking your hands off the steering wheel of life and joining your attention with life as it is. You mentally give up, surrender, throw in the towel and trust that your Spirit can guide you better than your heavy thought leaden mind can.

This is when that trust is needed. It is also when the decision is finally made, between flowing with life and continuing to struggle within the egos suffocating world of 'becoming'. At first it seems as if you would be sacrificing your current lifestyle in order to choose awakening, but *no* – you would actually be enhancing your enjoyment of life. If what the ego offers leads to discontentment, stress and unhappiness, then why would it be viewed as being a sacrifice to let it go? What good is it really, to gain the egos world, but lose the peace within your own soul?

But it all depends upon what you want. Do you *really* want to enjoy every moment of simple life, or would you rather trade that enjoyment in for a life of pursuing what your ego _thinks_ you need? The ego usually doesn't want to do anything in life, unless there is a payday at the end of it all. Working simply because you feel a deep urge to do something for the sheer joy of it, is totally incomprehensible to the ego. The ego views this kind of natural activity as being wasted time.

When you go with the flow of Spirit/Life, then you will find that your natural interests and talents will begin coming to the surface of your awareness again. I say _again_ because these natural interests and talents are probably something that were very much at the top of your awareness whenever you were a child or teenager, but you possibly threw them out at some point along the line, because you were too busy trying to '_become somebody_' within the egos world.

We all have these natural interests buried within us, and it is these which the Spirit will gladly support whenever we act upon them. Then life ceases being an up-hill struggle. Then we can take our hands off the steering wheel and enjoy the ride. We then don't feel it necessary to 'make our lives work' since when we follow our own true passions and interests, our life is already 'working' the way it was meant to work, with fun and with ease!

I theorize that if we were all educated correctly to begin with, then these natural inclinations would be encouraged and watered so that they could grow within us. If we were actually encouraged to pursue our own innate interests' then learning would be so much fun, and not only that, we would probably end up as being moderate Einstein's within the sphere of our fascination. We would then naturally go with the flow of life, and we would most likely live in union with God also. But usually our natural talents and interests' are stamped out and put down by the world around us, as we play the egoic game of follow the leader.

I recall one such moment in my own life. I remember I was sitting in school one day during a free class with a substitute teacher. I was thirteen years old, and I was flicking through a rather thick book I had borrowed from the library about the psychologist Sigmund Freud. I know it's a pretty strange thing to be reading at thirteen, but it interested me. Along came the teacher, and since the rest of the boys in the class were busy making noise and messing about, he stopped at my desk and asked what I was reading. So I told him, and his response was, *"You should put that psychology rubbish away, you won't get anywhere in this world with that, it's computers you want to be studying, that's where the real money is."*

Then off he walked, and being young and easily influenced, I did as he said. I put the book away and wasted my time struggling with computers for a while (which I disliked). But hey, all of these years later the natural interest in psychology is still there. Now, any decent teacher would've seen that I had a natural wiring for psychology and would've encouraged me to follow the path which I clearly loved. Years later, as I quit listening to know-it-alls and did follow my natural interests, I was able to start going with the flow of life. I was then able to finally let go of the struggle to 'become'. I gave up trying to 'make my life work' and I packed in the effort of trying to construct a better 'me'. Then I was able to live in Attentive Presence naturally and with ease, without effort or struggle, and life became a bit of an adventure as I flowed along doing the things I was naturally wired for. I done those things for the sheer fun they brought into my life, and for that reason only.

Only the thought leaden mind can interfere with our natural genetic wiring. Only the thought leaden mind causes division, separateness, struggle, war and all of the darkness in our world. Our natural interests will never produce problems or stir up trouble, only the thought leaden mind will do that. Some of the greatest inventors of our time have had their inventions hijacked by the worlds' sleepwalkers, and only *then* were these inventions used for dire purposes, much to the dismay of the inventors themselves. The inventors were clearly going with the flow, but the sleepwalkers weren't. So now for example, we have nuclear or atomic energy being used inappropriately.

The Spirit appears willing to support our

natural creature-hood, because then we are not going against the grain or introducing any effort; we are enjoying ourselves and what we are doing. We are then like creators, participating with life and God, like perpetual artists, moulding the fabric of life to our hearts fervour. That's what flowing with the Spirit is all about; and that's when the effortlessness of awakening becomes very apparent.

Making your life work:

At this moment I am reminded of something which a wise old Irish man once said; he said, *"Son, if you want to make God laugh, tell him what you are doing tomorrow."* Now, for an awakening to have lasting effect you just have to go with the flow of life, and where the flow don't go, you don't go, it's as simple as that. You see, with spiritual awakening, tomorrow does not often get a thought. Now don't get me wrong, you still keep a diary of appointments, but the hectic mapping and controlling of life tends to fall away from you. Many people live their lives like this. They try to maintain a tight grip upon every aspect of their lives, and it's something which just *can't* be done without stress and anxiety being introduced. These people remind me of those showbiz guys who try to keep plates spinning on top of long sticks. If there are too many plates spinning, it gets impossible to keep them all balanced, and then we find stress being introduced.

With awakening you stop controlling, you

quit chasing, you cease wanting and you begin to recognize that all is well, because then all is indeed well within your being. That feeling realization is then extended out into your world, making your outer world agreeable to you also. The old dissatisfied egoic mentality that once _refused_ to be happy until it had a fancy car or X amounts of money, just doesn't have a voice that you would want to listen to anymore. You can still drive a fancy car, don't get me wrong, I'm not suggesting that you should be driving an old rusty banger, or go around the place with holes in the backside of your trousers. But once awakened to the true Spirit of life, you won't be acquiring these things with an inferior need to make yourself feel good anymore. Your good feeling will be coming from within. It will be coming from the Spirit, and not from outside of you, and you will understand that nothing from the outside could ever make your life feel as sunny as the Spirit can.

There are many teachers out there, who will teach you how to take firm control of yourself and your life. They will teach you how to make a new ego for yourself. They have five year plans, lists of goals and targets to reach. They want you to delve into your unconscious to relive past hurts, to heal your inner child and to program your mind to 'become' a better 'you'. Yet all the while, the unconscious suggestion from this kind of activity, is that you are currently not good enough!

They don't seem to realize that past hurts, mistakes and bad experiences can bring a lot of wisdom in their wake. The effect of these past hurts can sometimes cause us to be willing to let go, into the moment, and surrender to the flow of life. The influence of our 'past hurts' can be released in the present moment; however it requires for us to allow our awareness to clear. A spiritual teacher I once visited made a very powerful statement, he said to me, *"living in the present puts an end to the past, and it dissolves all of your past hurts automatically"*. Now try telling some of these 'make your life work' teachers that!

I call these teachers the 'make your life work' brigade. The 'make your life work' brigade is generally a very decent kind of breed. They are trying to help people to improve their lot in life and that's good, but they have now infiltrated the spiritual seeking world. What they teach sometimes brings in an element of the universal source energy, and many spiritual seekers are attracted to their discourses. So what happens when _sincere_ spiritual seekers are attracted to the 'make your life work' brigade? Once attracted, the spiritual seeker usually stops seeking the Spirit _within_ and they cast their eyes _out_. They focus upon the exterior life, and lose all focus of the interior life. They forget that when the interior is _enlivened_, then the exterior automatically follows and gets enlivened also. They lose sight of that pure realization, which they were really interested in from the outset. Yet apparently seekers are interested in the Spirit and knowing it intimately within their own experience. But if you get caught up with the 'make your life work' brigade, then you will most assuredly get distracted from awakening to that Spirit within. You will also get distracted from going with the flow of life, which is so intrinsic to spiritual awakening.

I am often faced with the 'make your life work' brigade, and they are generally a nice bunch of people. However they don't appear to be at all interested whenever I try to explain to them that I like to go with the flow of life. It's almost as if they misunderstand what I am saying; taking it to mean that I prefer to sit around all day sunbathing or strolling up and down the local seaside promenade like a beach bum. They don't want to listen when I tell them that I do indeed _act_ upon the guidance or intuition I receive from within, and I don't just wait around for some unseen hand to carry out the actions for me. So I find it easier to tell these guys the following - _'Look mate, I go with the flow, and where the flow don't go, I don't go!'_

You see, I perceive that all is well within my world, and I have an innate knowing which allows me to know that all is going to remain well within my world. I realize that my exterior world is experienced according to the state of my inner nature. Now, my inner nature is in alignment with my true nature as Spirit. Therefore, I perceive the exterior world as being that which is the very same _one thing_ as my inner essence - i.e. _Spirit!_

I am no longer bound by the hypnotic spell of

thought, so therefore I am no longer trying to run away from any inferior feelings, nor do I feel the need to 'become' something that I am not. I don't have the _want_ anymore, to 'become' something which has been formed by societies clone like thinking. I can't see the point in maintaining an illusory ego or an outward face which is sterile and practiced, just so the world will maybe think some good thoughts about me. I no longer care what the world thinks about me, because it only matters what I think, since what I think is the only thing which has any power to alter my perception of the world I know.

When we take care of our interior life, then our exterior life tends to take care of itself, since our exterior life is nothing more than a great projection of what lies within us. Now if what we are allowing to be expressed within our awareness is the Spirit, then we are going to see that very same Spirit all around us also, since our inner state is projected as our outer world.

The experience of the Spirit is that _all is well_, and we then see the world according to that perception. Yes even when problems arise, all is still well. Problems are taken care of to the best of our ability, but they no longer cause us mental turmoil. So when we see and feel that all is well, then we don't feel the need any longer to fix what we once thought of as being un-well. In short, we no longer perceive anything as being broken, so we don't feel the need to fix what we cannot see as being broken.

So therefore, we don't see that we need to 'make our lives work', because we know firsthand that the only reason we ever felt the need to 'make our lives work', was because we were saturating our awareness with thoughts of an inferior and lacking quality. When those thoughts are ignored and we allow instead the emergence of the Spirit; then that perception of inferiority and lack is gone. The abundant perception of the Spirit gets projected into our world, and it is then that we will feel that all is well.

Someone once said to me, whenever they realized that my priority interest was in awakening to Reality; *"Ach, all of these spiritual guys, chasing after spirits whilst letting their lives go to waste."*

Now, it seems to be the case, that those who have released their grip from the steering wheel of life and have allowed themselves to awaken to the spiritual Reality, all find that going with the flow of life works much better than trying with effort to 'make your life work'. By going with the flow you enjoy all aspects of life, and no longer demand anything from life. You no longer have that clinging, needy and impoverished state of mind, which once made you feel so small. So I don't know about you, but I *can't* call that 'letting your life go to waste'. However, I would call living your life in total dissatisfaction and stress - letting your Life/Spirit go to waste!

Now, your life will never 'work' whilst you remain in stress, and it doesn't matter how much money you make throughout your life, because with that stressful, demanding and dissatisfied attitude of mind, you will never be able to enjoy life anyway. You'll be too busy coping with your stress. Now, that is _not_ making your life work - that is ruining your life!

All the same, whilst going with the flow we have to be alert to the inner inspiration and urges we may receive from the Spirit. And when we do receive it, we have to _act_ upon it. But don't worry, the acting won't feel like a struggle or effort, because when that which inspires you from within makes itself known, the way to follow will be plain sailing, and you'll have a great old pleasing time into the bargain.

Nonetheless, if you know that you are not _truly_ going to surrender and flow with Reality and the Spirit, then stick to the 'make your life work' brigade, because who knows, what they teach may eventually work for you. The guys who teach the hundred ways to a better 'you' stuff will certainly think so anyway!

10

Taking a Chill Pill

Spiritual practice:

I recall a time when I was studying to become a Yoga teacher, I was struck one day by how serious and almost poker faced many of the aspiring Yoga teachers in my class were about their disciplines and practices. To me, Yoga was all about attaining enlightenment, and enlightenment was the be all and end all of life as far as I was concerned, so I too was rather serious when it came to things like Yoga practice and meditation.

However, on one particular day in the Yoga class, a light switched on in my mind as I looked about the room at the other wannabe teachers. We were all gathered together, about fifty of us in all, and we were receiving instruction in a rather uncomfortable breathing practice by a visiting Indian Yogi. Everyone was sitting on the floor cross legged, with straight backs, eyes partially closed and focusing on this uncomfortable breathing practice for what seemed like infinity.

I hated some of the breathing practices they taught us in Yoga. A few of them were very useful for relaxation and calming down, but some of them seemed to be plain ridiculous, they just made my chest feel like a vice grip was crushing it. So despite being told that this particular breathing practice was going to help increase my 'prana' (life-force) and aid in my eventual 'enlightenment', I stopped the practice after about twenty minutes and instead looked around me as everyone else got on with it.

As I sat there, I found myself reflecting on why all of this meditation, breathing and Yoga practice wasn't producing any enlightenment in anyone I knew of. Of course, they always promised that these practices *would* result in eventual enlightenment, but the evidence to back this up was in short supply.

In my mind, and in all of the enlightenment teachings I had heard of, enlightenment was said to bring a state of joy, light heartedness, ease and a letting go of all effort to become. But as I gazed around the room, I noticed for the first time that there were no signs of 'ease' and 'letting go' in evidence amongst the aspiring Yoga teachers I was mingling with. There was a lot of stringent control in evidence, but certainly no joy, ease or letting go. Around this time, I was even caught up far too much with various practices, philosophies and techniques, and I was way too much involved in trying to control myself to feel any ease or peace within. As I looked around the room, it became clear that all of my fellow students were the same. We were all like robots, programmed with our philosophies, our practices and our stereotype 'Yogi' lifestyles far too much, to even dare to let go, take it easy and chill out.

Whilst I was noticing all of this, I wondered for the first time, if I was maybe wasting my time with all of these practices. Spiritual philosophies and their related practices, were leading me to take life way too seriously to leave any room for simple fun. Along with the philosophies came the list of spiritual rules one had to abide by, which seemed to suck all the juice out of life. We aspiring 'Yogis' usually got tangled up in a mess of heady philosophy as we tried to make sense out of life, creation, living and dying and what God was really all about etc.

Whilst sitting straight backed and cross legged in the Yoga class on that particular day, with an ever increasing discomfort in my lower back, I pondered over all of this. Then I heard one of my Yoga friends sniggering to herself on my right. I looked round and she too had her eyes opened, but with her hands clasped over her mouth as she tried to stifle her laughter. Finally she got 'control' of herself, and so I leaned over and whispered to her, asking what she was laughing at. She responded with, *"My God look at them all, they all look so uptight, why can't they just lighten-up?"*

She was right of course, after all, Yoga was supposed to help people relax, unwind, find inner peace, move more freely and ultimately find spiritual union, which is what the word Yoga points to. But if it was going to produce a deathly serious person who lived their lives by a list of stringent practices, then it was *certainly* not bringing what it promised. I then allowed myself to laugh at my friends' observation, but partly laughing at myself also for being so rigid and controlling.

Now, in Yoga they use the word 'Atman' to refer to the inner Spirit. There was a theory that all of the practices in Yoga were said to unleash or make known this 'Atman' within ones awareness. So my Yoga friend leaned over to me a second time, still sniggering as she passed comment on this Atman theory; she whispered, *"I don't know about you, but there's no sign of my Atman appearing on the scene today, in fact, with all this breathing going on, I think my Atman has left the building"*.

At that we both burst out laughing, much to the dismay of our fellow students and the Indian Yogi we had teaching us. If looks could kill, then we would've both been dead on that particular day.

If enlightenment or spiritual awakening was said to be the way to true ease, peace and happiness, then why did ease, peace and happiness get the boot whenever spiritual seekers grouped together? I can't figure it out. Certainly life isn't meant to be stifled with all of these spiritual practices, is it? To uncover our true nature, surely we don't have to practice anything, do we? After all, if it takes a practice to become aware of our natural state, then that natural-ness couldn't be said to be very natural, now can it? Well, if it's natural, then it can't take effort or practice to realize it!

I finally noticed that the good old ego enjoys a nice little practice, because practice always means that you won't 'arrive' at your awakening until _tomorrow_, whenever you become 'good enough'. And of course, to the ego you'll never be good enough for awakening, because to stand up and shout at the world, _"Heh, I am good enough"_, is seen as being the height of arrogance in the eyes of the worlds' sleepwalkers.

To those who wish to remain asleep, your awakening is seen as being a threat to their dream world, to their little 'me', to their sense of victimhood and to their desire for drama. Your awakening means that humanity is not the lowly species we all like to think we are. It means that the power is really in our hands to transform this world. It means that we will have to stop blaming others and blaming God, for all of the problems we supposedly face.

Yes _your_ awakening is seen as a threat, even to many posing as spiritual seekers, and that's why we have a multitude of practices to sift through whenever we take to spirituality. Practice always means _future_ and since awakening happens in the here and now, then it cannot possibly take a practice to allow it to happen. You don't have to practice to become aware of your natural-ness. Just let yourself be, give up your philosophizing and all of your spiritual manipulation, and all of your endless games of becoming.

Why not take a chill pill for a change? Align your attention with the here and now, with your senses alive. Pay attention to life as it is happening right now! Let your senses savour life; look, listen, feel, taste and smell life – *Now, Now and Now!*

This is certainly no practice. Filling your mind up with trash thought dramas takes practice, it takes work and it is truly damn tiring. But taking your attention out of thought and aligning your attention with the here and now - well, this is natural, and this is how we all lived once as very small children, before we allowed our attention to go to sleep in the dream world. Sleeping in the dreams of thought need no longer be the case however.

Right now, you could tie up your attention with life, just as it is happening right in front of you, in this and every moment. Snap the spell of thought which locks your attention into a semi dream world, and awaken with Attentive Presence to the ever present Reality which never leaves you.

Your *attention* is the key. Now what are you being attentive to, thought or life? Be daring, go on, allow yourself to wake up out of the thought world, and emerge fully alive into the *Real* world, where the Spirit and the true unity that is God can be found.

The desire to get real:

As the years progressed from my Yoga teaching days, I gradually moved away from all practices.

Eventually I gave up on all philosophies and belief systems also. I realized that philosophy and belief systems were only thought, and since I wanted to move _beyond_ all thought, they were of no use to me anymore. Indeed, they never were of any use to me anyway, since I didn't want spiritual entertainment, I wanted Reality. However, I still remained a little naive enough to discuss my new and uncompromising desire for Reality with other spiritual seekers. This usually upset them. They would then attempt a version of saving my soul, which meant that I would be expected to accept _their_ second hand philosophy, guru or beliefs etc.

To this day, I still occasionally come across folk who wish to 'save' my soul. These people think that I'm lost without their philosophies and beliefs. They are always trying to spiritually educate me. When I mention how simple it is to awaken from the thought trance whenever we _truly_ desire it, I usually get a reaction as if I have blasphemed or committed an atrocious 'sin'. Silly 'me', sometimes even I momentarily forget how much seekers are addicted to their spiritual practices, philosophies and beliefs, or better put - to thought!

"Oh well", I often say to myself, _"I'll leave them in their little dreams, and I'll continue to go on my ease, flowing in every moment with the care-free current of Life"_.

I guess some folk just don't want to look out from under their heavy baggage of belief and philosophy, to _dare_ to consider that maybe awakening is simple after all. But like I said, it's only simple when you truly desire it, more than your wandering mind. When that desire is firmly in place, then you'll not need the likes of me to tell you what needs letting go of, because when that burning desire to get *real* takes over you, then you'll find aligning your attention with the Reality of the here and now to be a natural thing.

Now, I know what you are wondering at this moment – is there a practice I can 'do' to hasten that desire into place? Well the answer is an absolute no! Either you are an adventurous person who is thrilled with the prospects of awakening, or maybe you have reached the end of your tether with the day dreaming mind. Usually it's one or the other before you will <u>*totally desire*</u> a switch into Reality. Most people just love the mind wandering entertainment of thought far too much to want to let it go.

Unfortunately, I have noticed that most people don't want to get real about awakening, until they have practically driven themselves over a precipice, into a state of hell mind. And, as startling as it sounds, some folk, when in that state of hell mind, still make excuses and come up with reasons why they can't or won't move beyond it. To my observations, it appears that some people actually *want* to live in a state of hell mind, and they also want everyone else to live with them there.

So, with awakening, I would say that you have to desire it above all else. You have to be willing to let go of your victimhood, and accept responsibility for your own mind. You have to be willing to get *Real* with yourself. The strength of your desire is the fuel which will keep you awake permanently. Without that, the best you can hope for is a momentary spiritual experience every now and then.

Now, don't think I'm knocking spiritual experiences. Spiritual experiences are nice, and can sometimes be quite powerful, it's certainly better to have them than not to have them, but a fleeting experience is not what awakening is all about, you have to understand this. Once awake, you'll probably not care much about spiritual experiences anymore, even though they do come more frequently. Most of the time there's just a great clarity, and a sense of unity with everything you gaze upon. Because of this clarity, as you look at the world, you will feel like you are looking at yourself a lot of the time.

So awakening is not about experiences, it's also not all about gathering lots of beliefs and philosophies. It's not about reading books and chasing gurus. It's not about acting spiritual or being a good guy either. It's about _awakening_ out of your thought trance and seeing Reality as it is, and not as you _think_ it is. Then you will no longer be a slave to thought. You'll be free of the mental burden which most of humanity falls prey to. You'll know what you *really* are, and will no longer be fooled with what you think you are. You'll live in peaceful freedom, a slave to no one, a slave to no spiritual rules, philosophies, beliefs or gurus. You'll be a Reality man/woman, and no longer a sleepwalker. Then you'll be your own master, paddling your own canoe and singing your own merry little song of life.

But come on now, you decide; do you *really* want to trade in your thought dramas for Reality? Why not make this moment right _now_ your crunch time for decision? Do you really desire the awakening of your inner truth? I find that most seekers don't want to trade in their philosophies, beliefs, gurus and thought dramas for Reality. They are just happy to be seekers, and that's okay. It's as valid a pass-time as any other the world has on offer. However, throughout the years as I encountered various teachers and many other spiritual seekers, I noticed that all one had to do to upset these people, would be to simply disagree with their spiritual beliefs or philosophies. I found myself wondering, *"Where's the happy, peaceful and playful expression of Spirit that enlightenment is supposed to bring?"*

Philosophy & guru addiction:

Being glued to a particular philosophy or belief system, and indeed guru addiction, are very difficult traps to get out of. They can be detrimental to one who is seeking awakening. Indeed, after awakening I became increasingly aware that to many seekers, spiritual awakening was all about revering the guru, rather than actually taking on board what he was teaching and using it to benefit one's life. After all, a guru is only a teacher and a human being just like any of us, but because we dream up all manner of strange associations about what it means to be awakened, we end up looking upon these gurus as if they are superior. I've heard of many gurus who are regarded by many as being incarnations of God, but what we don't seem to appreciate is this little fact, _we are all incarnations of God_. Everyone and everything is an incarnation of God!

God is the great totality, the non-dual crux of all life, of all worlds, of all dimensions and of all Reality. Awakening brings this truth into ones awareness, and that is the _only time_ when you will know this for sure - when you realize it in your own awareness! You may believe or disbelieve it, but your belief or disbelief is meaningless without the realization in your own awareness. When you allow yourself to realize this truth _first hand_, then and only then can you really go beyond all belief. Until that moment you may use belief as a comfort mechanism, and heh that's okay, there's no harm in that, just as long as you don't go out and do what many others have done with their comfort mechanisms, like burn someone at the stake, kick start a war or crucify someone who disagrees with you.

I have often noticed that many spiritual seekers revere their gurus so much, that they will even hang pictures of their favourite guru up in the house, and some will even light candles under the picture. It's a guru addiction they have, but most seekers don't see it as an addiction. They cling to the guru like lost little children, wanting someone to hold their hand and say, *"Don't worry, you don't have to take responsibility for your mind, I'll do it all for you"*.

Instead of letting go into the moment with ease, and going with the flow of the Spirit, seekers appear to want *more* control, more practices, more beliefs, more stressful 'becoming', more books, more teachers, more anything at all, just as long as they can continue living in the thought world. Yet most spiritual minded folk will take to spirituality because they want relief from stress, they want to be free from the burden of the egos world, they want peace, happiness and to feel at one with their world and fellow man. But usually they end up even more burdened, whenever they become entangled in a maze of philosophy and new age spiritual practices. They usually wind up losing sight of their original intention to awaken to their true inner spiritual nature, whenever they begin dabbling in the complex world of spiritual seeking.

Many spiritual seekers it appears, will then give up on attaining <u>true</u> spiritual awakening, and will settle instead for conforming to a spiritual stereotype image they hold in their minds. They try to live the stereotype 'spiritual' lifestyle. They will become vegetarian or an activist of some sort, they will get the sacred syllable OM tattooed onto their arm or they will attend satsang with the latest wise sounding guy who appears on the scene. All and any of this will do, just as long as it doesn't involve any true awakening, because who the hell would 'I' be without my thought manufactured 'spiritual' identity, huh?

This spiritual stereotype image of course, more often than not, leaves these people bound in the chains of many do's and don'ts. It leaves them caught up with more rules and regulations to live their lives by, than any religion could've ever imposed upon them. It leaves them as _slaves_ to someone else's idea of who and what they should be, but this is what most 'seekers' want.

It takes great control to live your life like this, but awakening involves the _relinquishment of all control_, and it requires a surrendering to the flow of life into the moment that is now. It requires for you to take a chill pill and let go. So, by burdening the mind with philosophy, beliefs, spiritual rules, practices and endless 'becoming', seekers are unknowingly taking a major step in the wrong direction – a direction which is the complete opposite to the awakening of peace, of joy, of light-heartedness and of spiritual freedom!

Happiness:

Many people will also take to spirituality because they want to find true and lasting happiness in life. But I wonder do we ever consider the real reason for our lack of happiness in the first place? Let's face it, if we are filling our mind up with thoughts of a paranoid, upsetting or depressing nature, then can we really not understand why we feel stressed, depressed, angry or despondent? Most of us never equate our own thinking as being the source of our stress and unhappiness. We usually look outside of ourselves, and blame other people or the world at large for the torture we place upon ourselves.

We run to the guru, because on some level we think that he is going to have a look inside our mind, and take all of the trash we have in there out for us. The guru is going to patch us up and then we will be nice and 'cured'. We believe that the guru is going to do it all for 'me'. Yet how can the guru keep _your mind_ clear and present in the moment? Only we can 'do' that; that is our responsibility, not the gurus. We are the ones who willingly fill our minds up with trash thoughts, and no guru anywhere in the world will ever be able to stop us from contaminating our own awareness with downbeat thought scenarios. No book will ever do it for us, no guru will ever do it for us and no spiritual path will ever do it for us, because we have to do this for ourselves. Only we can decide when we have had enough of the thought trash, and then choose Reality and our happiness instead.

All of the choices we make in life appear to be for the sole purpose of enabling us to experience some happiness, aren't they? I mean, isn't that supposed to be the big driving force behind all of our decisions, all of our ambitions and all of our wants in life? To be happy, that's the great big ideal, isn't it?

We want a good job so that we can make enough money to get all of those things we _think_ it takes to make us happy. That's why we may get married and have children etc. We go on holidays for the same reason; to have a few weeks of relaxation, peace and happiness, don't we? Spiritual practices are also supposed to bring about this state of abiding happiness. So we find ourselves doing many things in life, which are supposed to facilitate this great ideal of maintaining happiness. I have no doubt that *some* of the people who have done all of these things, have indeed found the happiness which was sought. But I'll bet that if you asked them where their happiness *really* came from, these are the very people who will tell you that their happiness is a state of mind.

At the time of this writing, Warren Buffett is one of the richest men in the world. During a lecture he once gave, he told his listeners that if they think their happiness will come from having a big house, big car or X amounts of money, then they are very much mistaken. He told them that when he earned $10,000 a year, he was just as happy then as he is now that he's amongst the worlds richest. He said that happiness is a state of mind, which comes as a result of doing what you love to do and what you are naturally wired for. He said that he always did what he loved to do (which happened to be playing about with the stock market). Now, Warren Buffett is a man who goes with the flow, and he sees his interest much like a game he is playing; he's obviously naturally wired for it. His flowing nature made him a billionaire, but Warren Buffett is renowned for not caring much about that. He still enjoys the simple things in life and there's no airs and graces with him.

Now, here is a man whom many would not consider at all to be a 'spiritual' person in the strictest sense. But upon observation, he's living a _real_ flowing kind of spiritual life anyway. It's plainly obvious if you studied this man, that he's only happy because of his attitude of mind, and because of his ability to play the game of life like the game it was meant to be. When you listen to him talk, you know that he's very much in the moment, flowing along, nearly always with a relaxed smile upon his lips. He was never interested in being anybody else other than himself, _just as he is!_ He dances his own dance, and sings his own song (so to speak), and he became highly successful in an _unattached_ way as a result of that attitude of mind.

A lot of folk who chase after all of the things they _think_ they need to be happy, appear to find that they still remain unfulfilled, despite treading all of the superficial routes which are supposed to bring lasting fulfilment and happiness in life. So, if the superficial routes we tread upon are found to fail in bringing the happiness and fulfilment which they promise, what then is it that we are actually supposed to do in order to bring about and maintain the happiness which we seek? What are we going to do when the superficial, and indeed the materialistic avenues of life have let us down?

Are we going to start living our lives in the

flow of the moment, doing what we love to do, activating our natural interests and talents and then playing them all like a game, just as someone like Warren Buffett does? Or will we continue to struggle through life, seeking amongst the superficial and materialistic world, believing that material things have the power to enliven us and make us forever happy?

In the attempt to 'make their lives work', even many spiritual seekers put themselves through hell, as they seek for peace and happiness. They struggle with spiritual disciplines and practices to get where they _think_ they want to be. And of course, after all of that struggle they are usually not happy, just rigidly addicted to philosophy and belief – so what was the point of it all we may ask? They spend many years of their lives _practicing_ how _not_ to be happy. Consider that even the Saddam Hussein's of this world, all did what they did because they wanted to be happy. Even if they went about it in some macabre and twisted ways, these people actually think that their struggle will have a glorious and victorious end, which will bring great happiness into their lives.

However, struggle and effort will never lead to happiness, because you are perpetually denying your _present_ source of inner happiness, by casting your happiness into the _future_. Only those who embrace their natural self and flow in the moment with the great game of life, much like Warren Buffett, can truly be happy, and can only accurately be said to be a *real* success in life. Allowing ourselves to be mentally at ease with each new day, no matter what is happening - now that's what *real* success is! When we flow in this manner, then there is no stress and no struggle to get where we think we want to be.

So you see, this is the importance of flowing with the current of life, in the moment, here and now, just being as you are, playing your game the way you are uniquely wired to play it. Sometimes you win and sometimes you lose, but you are unattached either way. That's the beauty of living your life in the moment; you generally don't consider that 'big scary future' which the rest of humanity is always talking about. This leaves us in a happy state; in a peaceful, care-free and naturally relaxed state, and then that opens one up for a spiritual awakening to take place.

11
Dialogues

Q: You say that philosophy and books can confuse us, but don't we have to read books or philosophy first, before we can find a way that works?

A: Yes, we do have to read some books or maybe listen to one or two teachers, because we need someone to point the way for us, but where does it all end? What happens after you read the book or listen to the teacher – do you awaken, or do you even use what you have read in those books at all? More often than not, most seekers usually read tons of books, and never ever get around to the waking up part. They usually settle for philosophy or beliefs instead.

I read tons of spiritual books during the years of my search, and at the end of it all, I didn't know whether I was coming or going. One book would say to do nothing, yet another book would tell you to meditate 2 or 3 times a day. Other books would suggest delving into the dark recesses of your unconscious, and others would have you trying to locate a hypnotist who could regress you into your past life to heal the illusive 'pain' there too. It can all get quite ridiculous really.

At the end of my search, I finally narrowed my focus down to a few books I had, which simplified the teachings of how thought and belief can contaminate our reality – they also simplified the teachings of presence for me. I finally _used_ what those few simple books suggested. But at that point in my search I was finally _ready_ to use what I had read. I was no longer satisfied with just thinking or talking about it all. I wanted freedom from the tormenting voice in my head. Now, that's all that is required before you will ever allow awakening to occur - _you have to want awakening more than you want the voice in your head_!

A complete beginner could awaken, immediately upon hearing their first clear teaching on awakening. It all depends upon how much you are willing to allow that shift in your attention from thought to Reality. In fact, I knew a man once who read _one_ book, and no more than one, and it resulted in his awakening. He was ready to let go and move beyond thought, that's all. So, it took no time for him, just the simple understanding that his own thinking was the problem, and that presence was the cure. When he realized this, he fully desired awakening more than his thought dramas. Thus, awakening was the result.

Q: That would be a rare case you're talking about though, wouldn't it be?

A: Maybe it is a rare case, simply because many who claim to want awakening, are more interested in reading and seeking, rather than simple finding. *They enjoy reading and talking all about spiritual sideshow topics far too much to be bothered with simple awakening. They read supposed 'channelled' books or seeming 'non-dual' books; they run to this guru or that spiritual workshop, or we have them trying to figure out how the universe came into existence – all and any of this will do, simply because it keeps the seeking game alive!*

Q: But what's wrong with that?

A: Nothing's wrong with that – as long as you don't end up hypnotized by it all. Trust me, if you really are interested in pure awakening, then you won't want to saturate your mind with a whole lot of old words and talk. You'll end up believing everything, but realizing nothing! *That's how you become hypnotized. It's easy to spot one who is hypnotized by second hand philosophy and beliefs. All you have to do is say something different from what they believe, and if they are hypnotized, they will react strongly or maybe even viciously. Now, if you go further, by pointing out the obvious flaws in some of their philosophies, or if you call into question the motivations of their favourite 'guru', as I have done in the past - well then, you will really need to run for cover.*

You know, I have had some *downright nasty* reactions from some so called 'spiritual' seekers, merely because I have tried to simplify awakening, by stripping away all of the glitzy trappings which surround the teachings of spiritual awakening. They really *hate* what I'm saying, and they don't like the common Joe Soap manner of my speech either, because they are far too used to sideshow teachers putting on a show for them. At times, it has made me feel like the world hasn't changed *at all* from the days of the 'holy' inquisition.

Some seekers think guys like me are trying to take away their treasured philosophies and belief systems, but I'm not *really*. I know that most spiritual seekers are not in the *slightest* bit interested in awakening; they are indeed interested in *something* alright, but just not moving beyond the dream, and that includes the spiritual dream. These types of seekers haven't reached that crunch time yet, simply because they aren't willing to be simpleminded.

Now, by simpleminded, I don't mean dumb or stupid; only simple within your mindset. Most folk want to philosophize, debate and seek forever, and that's okay, it *really* is, I always say, because it is just as valid a hobby as any other – but here we are talking about awakening, not hobbies. If those in search of <u>true</u> awakening could only keep everything simple, and keep their mind free from complexity and all of the intellectual head stuff, then they would awaken with great ease. So far, I've found that those who *do* awaken, are simply those who have reached a point where they have had their absolute fill of thought dramas – even the thought dramas of spiritual entertainment.

Q: Do you really think that only a few books could work for everybody?

A: It's not the books which bring enlightenment, but rather, your <u>readiness</u> to use what is in those books that brings it. Of course they would have to be good clear and simple books; not those books which go into all manner of spiritual sideshow topics. The sideshow topics might be very interesting to read about, but they have nothing whatsoever to do with what it really means to awaken – they usually leave you drifting along for years on end, delving into everything that sounds very 'spiritual', but then one day you realize that you have accumulated lots of head stuff, but no firsthand experience, never mind an authentic awakening.

I would suggest that you narrow your book load down to a few simple books which you find inspiring. I would suggest that you don't go *too* much beyond a few though, or you will definitely end up confused.

Q: But we still have to read until we find the technique or meditation that works, don't we?

A: I don't know if you are ready to hear the blatant and simple truth yet or not, but you have to realize that the only way which really works for <u>everybody</u> at the end of the day, is just simple *presence. Presence is the best way to meditate; really it's the only effective way to meditate, since you should be taking that presence into everything that you do. It's a 24-7 thing, you know?*

Now, this isn't only *my* teaching here; any decent teacher worth their salt will be saying the *exact* same thing. All meditation and spiritual practice is meant to facilitate the awakening of spiritual awareness as a 24-7 thing. Now, remaining present throughout each day is the only way to facilitate this 24-7 awakening of spiritual awareness. Reading philosophy won't do it, that's for sure. All philosophy will do is fill your mind with thought, and will convince you that you already know all about the true nature of your Reality, when you actually won't – you'll just _believe_ that you do.

If you made it a habit to live every moment of every day in absolute presence, then you'll really come to know your true spiritual nature. If you are relaxing or taking a nap, then relax or nap in presence, and if you are going for a walk or working hard, then walk and work hard in presence. It's a habit one develops quite quickly whenever it becomes the main _priority_ in your life. Making it the priority of your life is the best thing you can do for you and your life. You'll then see everything afresh, and relate to everything in life in a new and liberating way.

Q: Sometimes I have to deal with some very aggressive and obnoxious people; they get me down and I end up stressed in their company. I find that an uplifting spiritual book will steady me, and get me back on track.

A: Yes, some good books can certainly do that alright, but we can't keep relying upon books forever, now can we? There comes a day when we have to stand on our own two feet, and meet the world head on. The books only <u>point</u> to Reality or awakening, but it's up to us to use what these books say, otherwise they are a waste of paper, not to mention money. Whenever the road seems rocky, or whenever you are overwhelmed after dealing with an aggressive person, well then, by all means dip into an inspiring book, but remember to use what you read, or else what is the point in reading it at all?

Q: How do you usually deal with aggressive people?

A: I don't deal with them. I find them to be quite boring individuals.

Q: But we all have these people in our lives.

A: Yes we do, but I mainly ignore them as best I can. It's either that or I get away from about them. I don't have any interest in these boring types. These days I view aggressive people much in the same way as I would view an upsetting thought. I treat these people in the same way as I would treat that thought; I just ignore them.

Q: But sometimes they are really in my face, and it's hard to ignore them.

A: I know what you mean; sometimes listening to these types is a bit like hearing nails being scraped along a blackboard. We have to deal with these people as best we see fit. I prefer not to deal with them at all. There are far too many nice people in this world, for me to be bothered with these boring and aggressive people. I prefer to keep madness completely out of my mind. I like to keep my mind clear and present at all times, free of madness. Since I no longer tolerate madness in my own mind, I am certainly not going to tolerate it when others try to implant their madness into my mind.

However, I always say that nobody is a Superman. At times, I too find that listening to the monotonous blabber of these aggressive types can occasionally drain me a little. So, that's why I would suggest either ignoring them, or preferably getting away from about them. Generally, if you keep your mind free of thought dramas throughout the day, these types shouldn't get you down too much. It's really only if you carry what they say into your own mind, and then start thinking about it, that you end up getting upset or stressed. So try to remain in the present moment at all times, keep your own mind free of thought dramas, and you'll find that letting go of the melancholy madness of others won't seem so difficult.

Q: There are so many thoughts coming and going all of the time; how can we possibly clear them all away? It sounds like something only a super person could do.

A: I have some news for you; as long as you believe that awakening is a super human thing, then that very belief will stand in the way of your own awakening. That's why I suggest that you should examine some of your beliefs surrounding awakening. Those kind of beliefs will keep you chasing after awakening forever.

I remember how it is though; all of those familiar low feelings of victimhood we latch onto and find so easy to believe in – that *'we're not worthy'* mentality of the ego. Then because we <u>want</u> to believe that we are not worthy of our true divinity, we embark upon a never ending spiritual search. We will find a 'teacher' who will 'help us' to search down this 'road' and up that 'path', leading us towards even more confusion. But we don't really want to rock the boat or give up the past. No, we want tomorrow to be the same as yesterday; we want the familiarity of the old and not the freedom of the *Real*.

Truly awakening is a marvellous thing, but it is nothing that we can think of beforehand, i.e. - It is not what we might imagine it to be. On the surface appearance, nobody may recognize that an awakening has occurred for us, but on the inside we are free. We are free from the mental clutter we used to entertain ourselves with. But everyone expects awakening to look like what they have read about.

According to the worlds prevailing theories; when you are awakened you are supposed to become somebody else, and are no longer allowed to be your natural self. You have to smile all the time, speak quietly and walk slowly, drink no wine or eat no meat. You are supposed to conform to the spiritual stereotype - but that's slavery, not freedom!

Q: How can we keep our mind clear in every moment of life? That would be like practicing a technique indefinitely.

A: You don't need to practice anything to become aware of your own truth. If it's true then it doesn't need cultivating, just realized. You realize it when you leave your awareness clear of thought; then maybe there can be some room left in your awareness for the Spirit to be realized. You don't have to go around fighting with your thoughts you know; just ignore them, whether they are good or bad, and cast your attention out through your senses upon life instead.

This doesn't take practice, just a simple willingness or desire to let go of the mind clutter. Why would you want to hold onto that mind clutter anyway? Is it for entertainment purposes perhaps; maybe because it brings a little drama to an otherwise empty life? You know if people had a few more hobbies to get them out of the house, then they would have no need to be creating mental movies inside their heads to entertain themselves all the time. Could it be that we think we will become bored if we switched off the mental movies? Don't you see that thought is the cause of boredom? It is the sole source of all annoyance, stress and despondency in life. But some people are attached to all of that annoying stuff, they haven't had their fill of it yet – so on goes the dream until they do have their fill of it, if they ever do!

Once the scales of desire tip over from the desire to stay asleep to the desire for awakening, then keeping your mind clear becomes irrelevant, because you'll find that when the desire for awakening burns fiercely within you, you will automatically begin paying attention to the now quite effortlessly. When thought is ignored and disinterest sets in with regard to the content of thought, then the momentum of thought begins to wither away. It slows down all on its own, due to your lack of interest in it.

Q: But setting aside some quiet time to practice presence can still help to prepare for awakening, can it not?

A: The Real isn't something which is lurking outside of the everyday mundane life you know. You don't have to set aside time for this. With every task you do, the Real is always present there – you just aren't paying attention fully to what you are doing, that's all. Your attention is divided between the doing and what you are thinking about. Maybe you are shopping for groceries and instead of actually being there, fully attentive to the shop you are in (the sounds of the shop, the smells of the shop etc), you maybe have your attention locked up in some daydream or fantasy land of thought instead. Hence, the present Reality eludes you.

So pay full attention to the now of your doing (whatever it is) and there you will find the *Real*. It doesn't take practice; it just takes the desire to get real. What do you choose; thought or Reality? Which seems more enticing, staying asleep in your dreams of thought or awakening with absolute ease, into the present Reality of Spirit as it is, here and now? This isn't going to magically happen all on its own you know, despite what some teachers and gurus say.

You have to ask yourself the important question - do you really want this? If you find your thought content entertaining, then you won't allow your attention to shift out of that thought content, it's as simple as that. There is no harm in the thought content, just as long as it leans more towards happy dreams rather than depressing or stress riddled thought-mares. So, are you happy with your thought content? Do you find it entertaining to be day dreaming all day long? If you do, then you can forget about awakening, because you won't find enough desire to fuel the awakening of spiritual awareness. Without a desire for truth, the flame won't be kept burning.

Q: Can a spiritual practice not help to grow awareness of oneness within us?

A: You are already that oneness, and so is everyone and everything else. We do a great job of hiding from this truth. We make up spiritual rules and philosophies, religions and spiritual practices so that we can 'connect' to our true self, but the funny thing is that we are already connected with this Reality. It's so simple really. We are not usually aware of this interconnection, because our awareness is dozing in thought dreams instead. How can we be aware of anything real, whilst our awareness is clouded with the un-real?

When we ignore the thought dreams, then our awareness becomes pure again, and _pure_ awareness reflects Reality naturally. When awareness awakens out of the daydreams, then we become aware of what has always been within us and all around us. Spiritual practices can at best bring us some temporary spiritual experiences, which are nice to have, but true and lasting awakening only comes about as a result of our burning desire to be free in Reality. No practice can make us desire Reality over thought. We either desire it or we don't.

Q: It's all well and good sitting around talking about spirituality; anyone can talk about it, but it's a person's actions that really count, not their words.

A: Actually, true spirituality does not depend

upon actions or words; it's only about pure realization in one's own experience and that alone. This realization is a living aware presence, it's a fact, and it's the absolute truth of our being. It's not a thought generated act. In fact, putting on the 'holy' or 'spiritual' act, only ever serves to interfere with this realization. The so called 'spiritual' or 'holy' performance is what the world has been faced with for long enough now. The religions have kept this pretence up for millennia, and now the new age movement is falling into the same old trap.

The childish pictures we have in our minds of awakened guys being super 'good' fellas who walk slowly, talk softly, who hug trees, smile all the time, and pretend to like everybody in the world, is absolute nonsense. This 'holy' or 'spiritual' act has gotten old and tired; it's played out and downright hypocritical. If you're really interested in awakening to Reality, then you should leave the 'holy' act to the religions, egoic gurus and the spiritual entertainment seekers of the world. If you really want awakening, then you should join the ranks of the true and <u>authentic</u> Reality guys out there.

The 'holy' act, of trying to behave in the manner in which we think an awakened person should behave, is just ridiculous to anyone who has any of the lights on within their mind. When we pretend to be very 'holy' or 'spiritual' we cannot avoid being hypocritical. Since we are involved in judging our own behaviour, we cannot avoid judging the behaviour of others as being 'unspiritual'.

We usually begin this act by trying to become a spiritual stereotype person, because we mistakenly believe that becoming this stereotype will make us ready receptacles for spiritual realization. But we _already_ have that Spirit within us, so we are therefore currently - _now_ - receptacles holding Gods Spirit within us. Altering our behaviour, speech or lifestyle to imitate what we think spiritual looks like is a fool's game. Awakening has damn all to do with your behaviour, your words or your choice of lifestyle, but has everything to do with how clear your awareness is, or how cluttered with thought it is.

After awakening you will find that certain aspects of your mannerisms or lifestyle will change, but they will change _naturally_, it's not forced or pretended. Pretence will never make way for awakening; it will only get in the way because you are trying to alter yourself with thought in order to construct a new thought made spiritual identity, a new spiritual 'me' - a new 'spiritual' looking ego. Now that's a really boring old game to be playing, I know, trust me, I've been down that silly old joyless road.

Stop acting spiritual and realize that you are _already_ spiritual. Stop pretending, stop imitating and stop trying to become, become, become. Dare to let yourself be _real_ and let your awareness clear for a while, and just see what happens then. Consider this; if there was nobody in the world to watch you perform your 'spiritual' act, would you bother with it at all? Once your mind clears of trash thought, then the behaviour which once emanated from that thought also disappears, so you won't end up as a bad guy by letting go of this silly behaviour control.

Are you putting on a spiritual act for others to think some good thoughts about you? Is it important for you to be seen as being the stereotype spiritual person? If the answer to these two questions is *yes*, then you are lost in the egos game of becoming, and you are interfering with your true natural expression. You are interfering with the Spirits flowing nature. I've noticed that spiritual actors rarely ever let that game go.

Q: I feel awake most of the time, and I am nearly always aware of 'what is', but it still feels like maybe there is something else which I have to do.

A: That doesn't make any sense to me. If you feel awake and are always aware of 'what is', then you certainly wouldn't feel like there was something else to do. You would come to realize, that this is very natural whenever it is your <u>priority</u> in life. Remaining awake depends upon whether or not it is a priority, simply because staying in the here and now happens moment to moment, it's a 24-7 thing. It's a preference for Reality over cloud cuckoo land. If you have lots of other little 'priorities' more important than that, then you will allow your mind to become cluttered with all of those little scraps of nonsense.

By the way, the best thing you can do for others and your own life in general is to become clear and present in the now; first and foremost. You'll be a nicer person for others to be around, and your life will feel like it is running more smoothly. That's why it's better to put the cart before the horse with regard to your priorities. Some people feel like they are being selfish if they put their own sanity and peace of mind above everything else in life, but really it's the best thing you can do for everyone and everything in your life. Insane or unstable people are usually not very nice people to be around, and they usually screw everything up also. Now, you are either awake or you are not, you say you feel awake most of the time, well which is it?

Q: Well, at times I feel energy moving in my body. There are different spiritual experiences I have had, although they don't last very long. That's why I wonder if maybe there is something else I need to do.

A: Many people feel like they are awake just because they have had some momentary spiritual experiences. But I've noticed that seekers tend to chase after spiritual experiences in the same way that a junkie chases after their fix of drugs. This leaves you like a prisoner; a slave to the addiction of spiritual experiences. Are you a spiritual addict looking for your fix?

I think you are confusing an experience with being awake. Awakening does indeed bring what could be called a new flavour of 'experience' into one's life; a fresher, cleaner, unifying, crystal clear clarity of perception, but it isn't like an experience which comes and goes. This clarity remains as long as we don't slip back into La La Land. Because of that clarity of mind, spiritual experiences will certainly come and go more frequently, but because of their impermanent nature, one should not really get all that hung up on them.

If you were really awake, then you would no longer be looking for anything else to 'do'. You only think there is more to 'do', because we have been conditioned to believe that awakening is about achieving some fixed and static blissfully energetic state. Nobody - and I repeat *nobody*, remains in a fixed state of bliss mixed with ecstatic energetic experiences all the time, and anyone who says that they do is a liar!

We think awakening has to do with kundalini experiences, or seeing auras and celestial beings, being psychic, mind reading, walking through walls or levitating. Now I feel it is high time that we supposed 'adults' should wake up out of all that silly nonsense. Awakening has absolutely nothing to do with these temporary experiences. Awakening really has to do with simply staying free of the thought spell and living in the *Real* world, where true unity is to be found.

I've met many people who have had pretty powerful and energetic spiritual experiences, and they still remain as total slaves to thought. This is simply because, after the experience wore off, they still found the thought spell to be so damn alluring. I think many spiritual teachers fall into that category.

There is absolutely nothing you have to *'do'* to wake up, you know? Paying attention to the moment is not something which needs to be 'done'. It's a mode of living and operating; it's a mode of being. Filling your mind up with a whole lot of old nonsensical thought scenarios takes a hell of a lot of 'doing'. With awakening you actually <u>cease</u> your constant and never ending mental 'doing', as you allow your attention to shift casually and effortlessly into the present moment.

Q: I don't think it's as easy as that.

A: Well then – As you think, so shall it be! When someone says to me, "it's not as easy as that", then I know that I'm talking to someone who has either become confused through listening to far too many spiritual sideshow teachers, or to someone who is just looking for an excuse to remain asleep in dream land. You don't need an excuse to remain in dream land, you know? It's your mind and your life; it's nobody else's business what you allow your awareness to be filled with. If you are enjoying your dream land, then that's okay, but if you are <u>really</u> interested in awakening, then quit with the lame excuses and allow realization to occur in your awareness, once and for all.

If it is lack of understanding you suffer from, then ask yourself this question - Is paying attention to life as it is happening right now, really all that difficult? Is it difficult to pay attention? It takes more effort to live in La La Land, you know. It takes no effort at all to stop and live in peace. Peace and effort cannot go together; it doesn't even make sense to say that it takes effort to find peace of mind. Effort is equal to stress. The cessation of effort is equal to perfect equanimity and peace. Is it really that difficult to simply stop and live in the here and now – to drink through your senses all that life brings, moment to moment?

Q: Didn't you have to spend over ten years searching before you finally awakened?

A: I spent over ten years wasting my time, because I was so fascinated with the whole spiritual sideshow malarkey. I spent ten years burdening my mind with second hand philosophies, beliefs and spiritual rules of becoming. I listened to far too many cranks and spiritual sideshow teachers. I chased after the temporary spiritual highs. I was a stereotype new ager. But all of that stuff only ever served to get in my way, even though seekers like to think that it all helps. That mish mash of new age and spiritual philosophy leaves the mind confused, thinking that it already knows what awakening is, when it actually doesn't.

It was thanks to a few simple teachers at the end of my search, who helped me see what I was doing to my mind. It wasn't until I got fed up with the thought dramas in my mind, that I finally let them go and switched into Reality. That didn't take any time; it just took a _willingness_ to get real once and for all. I then threw out all of the philosophies, the beliefs, the sideshow gurus and every other thing I burdened my mind with. In short - I threw out all thought dramas!

I asked myself that question - Is it really that difficult to simply stop with the effort, and live in the here and now? When I let go of my second hand belief system, I found that living for the moment wasn't difficult at all, it only appeared to be, because I was too busy philosophizing about it all. So you should stop your philosophizing, stop your gathering of second hand beliefs; stop thinking and start living, it's as easy as that!

Q: With a very busy routine in life, sometimes I wonder if I stopped, would the world stop too.

A: Yes, been there, got the t-shirt. You equate physical action with mental doing. You think that you need to have your mind racing, just because your body is working hard or fast. You don't have to stop physically, in order to keep your attention in the here and now, you know. We all have this silly picture in our mind, of the spiritual guy sitting cross legged on top of a mountain in total solitude, and we think, that's what it will take for me to allow the mental traffic to quieten down. That's all nonsense of course.

However, it does take a little _trust_ to let go of the mind stuff, to hand the reigns over to the Spirit, or life flow instead. Trust me, when you mentally give up and begin to live life in the moment, you'll get more done, and the quality of what you do will be much better. You'll also be able to go at it like a work horse, with more energy, better efficiency and still have energy to spare when you're done with whatever it is that you are doing.

You just got to understand that mental noise interferes with your life and everything that you do. It poisons everything, from relationships, to things you want to achieve; it makes enemies out of innocent people and ruins your level of happiness also. If you can only trust that the Spirit can do things much better than a mind which is filled up with trash thought, then letting go into the now moment should be effortless for you.

Q: Maybe we just need to say "to hell with it" in a very loud voice, and then we will awaken.

A: I like your style. Yes, just say "to hell with it", to the whole lot of it; all of the silly stuff which keeps your mind spinning out of control. What else is there to say to that kind of trash? I guess you could call that the modern vernacular for surrender. However, most people don't like letting go in this way. They like getting themselves all dirty from rolling around in the mental trash heap. It makes their lives seem a little less boring, like something is happening all the time. Inside their mind they have their own private soap opera running 24-7; their little story titled 'The Adventures of Me'. I suppose it's only when we have had enough of rolling around in the trash heap that we will allow ourselves to surrender, and then say "to hell with it".

Q: I've heard it said that awakened people usually abandon normal life, like family, friends etc, after awakening occurs. They usually live a more reclusive kind of life – is that true?

A: After awakening you will go with the flow of life, and where the flow don't go, you don't go. So whatever happens is whatever happens, you are done manipulating life or trying to control it. There's no more rules, no more stereotypical behaviour. You are life, simply flowing along at your ease. Sometimes you may find that things will change, but they may remain the same. You may change your job or not. You may move house or not. You may find yourself socializing with different people or not.

The outer life may not change at all, or then again, it might. There is no fixed stereotypical scenario which will play itself out. Life goes on and things happen, just as normal. People come into your life, and people go out of it. This is the same for everyone. My outer life hasn't changed a lot. I'm more active now, whereas beforehand I was somewhat lazy. I found that strange, since I once upon a time, thought that awakened folk sat around all day in a meditative posture doing damn all. I used to think that awakened people packed their job in, and lived saintly lives up in the hills. I live in absolute freedom now, and I do whatever I feel like doing. Of course, what I now feel like doing won't cause any harm for others. Since I am no longer harming myself through thought dramas, I won't be harming anyone else.

Q: From all that you are saying, it seems that what we have been searching for has always been the case, and we just weren't looking in the right place.

A: Yes, very well put, that's about the height of it. We have had our noses stuck in books galore; as if our true nature could ever be found inside a book. We have been trying to figure out Reality with thought, through our philosophies, our religions and our beliefs. We have been searching for gurus and all manner of wise guys to bow down to. We have been waiting upon a temporary ecstatic experience of transcendental bliss and euphoria etc. Yet no temporary experience will ever have a lasting effect; it always fades leaving us wondering, where did it all go wrong? We have been trying to imitate the awakened, by acting out the stereotypes of how we think the awakened should behave. We have been amusing ourselves with constant seeking, and more importantly, we have been amusing ourselves with constant thought dramas.

But it's all just thought dramas at the end of the day; all of this distraction I've mentioned. We have been distracted by so many religious and so called 'spiritual' thought dramas. We have allowed our awareness to become hypnotized by second hand belief systems. We have allowed ourselves to become like puppets on a string, dancing to the hypnotic melody of religion or the gurus' words, words, words and endless words.

And all the while, the *Real* no-thing that we are has been here all along, just waiting for us to recognize it once again.

So yes, we haven't been looking in the right place, we have been looking everywhere else *apart* from the right place. Yet the present moment, where Reality is to be found, is always here, right under our noses. The Spirit has always been within us, trying to illuminate our awareness with its essence, but we have lots of other stuff taking up space in our awareness, don't we? With all of the thought dramas we hold onto, what room will there ever be in our awareness, to know anything else but those thought dramas?

So, most spiritual seekers are certainly seeking for something, but with most, that something is certainly not *thee* Reality. However, Reality is always the case; and even logically, it can only ever be discovered in the here and now, that present moment which all true spiritual teachers talk about. There's nothing to 'become' in order to be aware of your truth. There's no purification needed to be in alignment with your natural self. No effort, no discipline, no practice. That truth is with you even as you hear these words. It's there within you and all around you, whether you believe me or disbelieve me. It will emerge into your awareness when you leave some space for it. So go ahead now, divert your attention out of thought and see this moment as it is - listen to this moment as it is - feel this moment as it is - smell and taste this moment as it is, and now - *behold Reality!*

The awakening of spiritual awareness arises as you pay attention to the here and now. It arises as you divert your attention to simple everyday life, as it is happening all around you. Reality is always there, with every breath you take, and with every move you make - and that's just how the song goes!

Meditation/Spirituality/Philosophy

This in-depth book delivers the psychology behind spiritual awakening in a thorough, penetrating and yet simple manner. The author Keith Loy aims to untangle the many heady philosophies which surround spiritual awakening, thereby liberating the seeker of awakening from the need for mere philosophy and belief. He hopes to lead the reader *beyond* belief and philosophy in all respects, in order to uncover the awakened state of spiritual awareness, right here, right now!

Keith has written this book for those who have grown weary of seeking and not finding. He demystifies and simplifies spiritual awakening, so it can now *finally* be accessible to all of those who truly desire it.

About the Author

As a devout spiritual seeker for over many years, Keith Loy encountered much of what confuses spiritual awakening. After what he views as being a long an unnecessary search, he finally managed to shake off all of the confusion he encountered, thereby allowing for the awakening to what he now simply calls Reality.

Lightning Source UK Ltd.
Milton Keynes UK
27 January 2011

166474UK00001B/31/P

9 781449 014551